FALL
INTO
HAPPINESS

An inspirational journey
through addiction,
abuse and loss

KAREN ALEXANDER

Fall Into Happiness/ ISBN 978-1-947398-01-6

Book interior design by Michele Uplinger

DEDICATION

This book is dedicated to my sons,
Blake and Brett Summers.
Thank you for your undying love and support
through my darkest days.
I would not be here today without your love.

To new beginnings and making memories together.
Always remember, "We got this!"

TABLE OF CONTENTS

CHAPTER I

BORN INTO CHAOS

My entire life I felt different, lonely, unfulfilled and unhappy. Unable to find peace in any situation. I settled in relationships, business and social affairs. I never felt good enough to live my dreams, passions, or to trust myself.

Surrounded by alcoholism, abuse and dysfunction, I thrived on living life as a charade. I knew what alcoholism looked like on others, but remained blind to my own addiction.

I destroyed relationships, my self-respect, business opportunities and, most importantly, my family. Rushing through life and justifying my actions by blaming others, running away, and—my favorite— numbing the pain, became my norm. I lived my life for over thirty years in the pretense of being successful and a good person.

From the outside, my life looked perfect: I had a beautiful family, a successful business, money, and fancy cars. Wearing only the latest fashions, with perfect hair and makeup, I played the part of a professional business woman, a happily married wife and devoted mother. I was none of those. Instead, I was an alcoholic, living a lie, experiencing a miserable existence.

My journey through addiction is filled with pain, struggle, and loss, but also hope and courage.

Raised in an alcoholic family, it's no wonder I married an alcoholic, for I never understood the power the disease of addiction holds over alcoholics and addicts until I became one myself. Every day, I told myself, was a new chance to start over, with a new plan to stop drinking. *Today* would be the day I would change—the day the pain, suffering and anger would end. When the attempts to change my life failed, that left me terrified. My calendar would be marked with an X for the days I drank and an O for the days I did not drink. I convinced myself tracking my drinking would help.

Instead, tracking only served to bring despair when I saw how many Xs were marked on my calendar. It was humiliating to see where my choices had brought me. I felt too ashamed to ask for help. How could I reveal my weakness, my struggles, and tell someone the truth? Telling the truth frightened me and was the real reason I didn't ask for help. I did not know how to be honest about what I needed.

Deep into my addiction to alcohol, the daily promises to quit drinking I made to myself and others would be broken by lunchtime. Sometimes by breakfast. Eventually, drinking around the clock became my life. Functioning on little sleep or food, my social life was over. No longer did I bother to make promises to myself or others. I stopped trying to control my drinking, resigning myself to a lonely, unhappy life.

My life had become so small, I thought there was no way out. Life without alcohol seemed a distant dream. I figured I'd live this way until the day I died.

At a young age, I learned to lie, to keep secrets, and—most damaging of all—how to deny my true feelings. I felt completely alone in a room full of people. Combine that with learning to accept unacceptable behavior from the people I loved and trusted the most, and a desolate pattern was created that shadowed me throughout my life.

My journey with alcohol and chaos began before I was born.

In the middle of a cold fall night in a small Wisconsin town, my father woke the family and told them all to get up and get dressed. In a panicked voice he told them, "We are leaving now!" No discussion took place, nor was there a plan . . . the family was simply to get in the car and leave the only home they knew. He packed up my two sisters and two brothers, ages two through nine, and my mother—who was pregnant with me at the time—and fled to California in an old beat-up station wagon.

My grandparents, aunts, uncles, cousins and friends were left without warning and without proper goodbyes. My sisters and brothers were not given a chance to say goodbye to their cousins or friends. They were heartbroken and petrified at what was happening, but could not speak up: they all knew something had happened and it was not good.

Speeding out of town, my father stopped by each grandparent's home to say goodbye. My grandparents cried and screamed, begging my father to change his mind and cursing him because he would not stay. They told my siblings they'd never see them again.

The pain and terror my brothers and sisters felt at that time had to have been powerful, yet they did not say a word. They held the pain inside and did what my father asked of them.

No one ever discussed why my father insisted the family leave home, friends, and family behind, but we all knew my father must have crossed the wrong people and had to flee.

One of my sisters later told me my family drove across country in silence, with the only the sounds those of sniffling from the tears of my mother and my sisters. My father drove silently and sweat profusely, perhaps from the treacherous Rocky Mountains or maybe from the trouble he had left behind. I'd imagine a little of both.

My family settled in a small town in Marin, California to start a new and better life—or so my father promised my mother. She cried every night from the pain of missing her mother and father. As her mother's only daughter, they were close and loved each other immensely. Family meant everything to Mom. Now she was alone in another state, with an alcoholic husband, four young children, and a new baby, for I was born a few months after they arrived in California. Terrified, alone, and broke. She'd married an alcoholic and was paying the steep price of that love.

My father's promise of a good life was soon forgotten. He found work as a bartender—great fun for him, but not so much for us children. My mother endured the most pain and struggle. She tried to hold us all together while watching the man she deeply loved obliterate their family.

Employed at a bar on the docks in San Francisco, my father worked and drank long hours with his so-called friends: longshoremen, teamsters, and drunken Catholic priests. He drank all day at the bar and, if he wanted to keep drinking, he would bring his friends home with him to continue the party. After midnight, they would come in the house, drunk and ready to whoop it up, showing little concern that five small children lay sleeping in their rooms.

The drunken Catholic priests, dressed in their Sunday best, would run through the house, blessing it with holy water. They'd come barreling into our rooms, chanting bible verses and throwing holy water on us in the middle of the night, to supposedly get rid of the evil in us.

As the night wore on and the alcohol ran out, fights began. They'd argue over nothing. Friends he barely knew yelled and bickered in our home. Then they took to the streets, men and women running around the block, some jumping in their cars and racing up and down the streets at three in the morning, yelling, swearing, honking car horns and waking the neighbors. This happened time and time again. We were the house on the block all the neighbors talked about. They wanted us to leave their previously quiet neighborhood.

When, occasionally, the neighbors tried to stop the noise, events would devolve into a good brawl in the middle of the street. Humiliated, I tried to avoid my neighbors. I just wanted my family to be happy and normal.

After such crazy nights, and only a few hours of sleep, it was hard to get up the next day for school.

The painful aftermath created such anger in the house. My brothers and sisters and I took this anger out on each other, bickering and fighting among ourselves. My older sisters talked about how they could not wait to be old enough to leave home. They both married and moved out by eighteen.

Filled with shame, I hated my home, and myself. I saw from a young age what alcohol did to people and swore never to be an alcoholic and never raise my children in such chaos.

I longed to be a normal girl like my friends, but didn't know how to be normal, how to feel, or how to treat others. I always felt everyone else knew how to live life but me.

My girlfriends had sleepovers and dinner parties for their friends. Their parents would buy special food, candy and games for all the girls, creating a lovely time for all of us. The fear of not being "enough" kept me from laughing and talking effortlessly like they did. I could not handle my feelings of not fitting in, so I usually pretended I was sick and went home.

Feelings of inadequacy, loneliness and unworthiness stole my childhood. I did not know how to *feel* in a peaceful environment. That kind of environment was foreign.

Even though my home was dysfunctional, depressing, and full of chaos, it was home and where I fit in. Sometimes we get comfortable in sadness and learn to accept it in our life.

Dreams of having sleepovers and dinner parties at my home were just, that—dreams. I never dared to ask to invite others over, for I knew what the answer would be. Our family had to live our lives around my father's drinking.

We were innocent children trying to find our way in life. How could my father rob us of peace and love? I wanted my father out of our lives.

One day, standing in the kitchen, I noticed a huge bread knife. I picked it up. My father was sitting at the kitchen table, saying horrible things to me, as usual. I thought, *just stab him. Life would be better if he was gone.* He must have sensed something, because he turned around to see me holding the knife. I put it down and left the room. I was ten.

After that day, I begged my mother: "Please divorce him."

My mother looked at me and said, "Honey, your father is sick. He has a disease. We need to take care of him."

My mother's words changed my perception of my father and of alcohol. I had never thought of him as being sick—I just thought he was a drunk and a bad father. But were we really supposed to take care of him? I must have taken this to heart because my whole life I excused bad behavior, thinking I could fix everyone. Truth was, though, I could not fix myself—but trying to fix others gave me a sense of relief. Focusing on them, I did not have to look inward.

One day at a friend's house, I was excited to go out and have fun with her. When she asked her mother for permission, I overheard her mother say, "No, you can't go with her. She's no good. She comes from a bad home with no discipline." My body filled with shame. Another reason for me to feel unworthy. Yet, I knew her mother was right.

Suffused with a feeling of worthlessness, I became a loner, not letting anyone get close to me. I wrapped myself in self-protection.

My mother was an amazing, affectionate person, so in love with my father. Witnessing their love when he was sober gave me hope as I tried to make sense of our family. My father was a good man—just like all of us are good people until addiction steals our morals, integrity and compassion for anything and anyone.

Occasionally, my father would stop drinking. When that happened, we were all warned: "Behave! Your father is on the wagon."

Not wanting to be the one to make my father drink, I would be the perfect little daughter. Thinking he would not drink if I was good, he broke my heart when he drank again because I thought he didn't love me enough to stop drinking. I was not worthy; my father did not love me. It was hard to bury my feelings but doing so became easier as I got older.

My sisters and brothers always knew his abstinence would not last and waited nervously for him to be drunk again.

It was only a matter of time before he would drive home completely drunk, speeding through the neighborhood, making a scene, the horn honking or the radio blasting. Once, he was given puppies at the bar from drinkers who had no money. The puppies would be climbing around him in the car as he flew through the neighborhood. Opening the car door to let the puppies out, we saw even they looked alarmed and thankful to get out of that car.

Many nights he drove home and landed on our lawn or in the middle of the street. Other nights he accidentally parked in the neighbor's garage. This led to fights with the neighbor. My father thought the neighbor was in his house when he parked in the neighbor's garage and proceeded into his home.

Going out to dinner was so frightening we never knew what to expect. He would get drunk and leave the table for the restroom. Once, after a long time had passed, we heard him yelling, "Where the hell is the restroom?" He was standing right in front of the restroom door.

Our family vacations were a disaster, too. We would be so excited to go camping or to a beach. Finally, we would reach our destination and my father would be so drunk he would pass out and leave my poor mother to find her way to the next stop. We had to push him into the passenger seat of the car as he yelled and made a scene. My mother had no idea where she was, plus she had a car full of rambunctious children, so she would drive aimlessly as my father lay passed out in the passenger's seat. He'd come to now and then to tell us off or yell at my mother, "Where the hell are we?"

Eventually, we would have to pull over to stay at a budget hotel. One night in a hotel pool the bugs were so big we had to dive under the water to get away. As kids you have fun, you make the best of a terrible situation, but we knew inside this was not good.

Life went on, with some good days, some bad days, but there was always a black hole inside me that I could not fill. No joy would last, no birthday would be sufficient. Nothing, no one, could fill that black hole in my soul. How did I have so much darkness at such a young age? I often asked myself, *why am I so bad?*

One day in sixth grade, I baked a cake for my teacher because she was moving away. My classmates and I loved her and planned a going-away party. Proud of my cake, I showed it to my father.

He looked at it and said, "You're stupid. You can't even spell." You will never be anything good.

I had written on the cake, "We'll miss you" instead of "We will miss you" to take up less space. Even though he was wrong—there is nothing incorrect about "We'll" replacing "We will"—his words followed me throughout my life. To this day they still sting.

It became a bad habit to disregard the positive things people said and instead hang onto the negative remarks.

The idea of being stupid filled me with shame. To avoid being thought foolish, I would never speak out loud in class or in business. I always second-guessed myself. To be smart was something I wanted all my life, but I thought I was not intelligent. I missed many opportunities in my life because I did not have any self-worth. Words are damaging and can never be taken back. We do not realize the damage we do to our family, friends, and especially our children when we use hateful words. When we are in our disease we are miserable . . . and want others to feel the same.

I knew all of this; however, I grew up and did exactly what I swore not to do: I became an alcoholic. And I raised my children in the chaos of alcoholism.

CHAPTER 2

THE LOSS OF INNOCENCE

L iving in the relentless turmoil of my childhood, I searched for ways to feel good, to fit in, to relax and enjoy life.

Daydreaming about being happy and carefree, but never knowing how to achieve that feeling felt frustrating. Then one memorable day it all changed. My life seemed to catch on fire. From that day forward, I ran through life with a flame burning bright inside, believing I could do anything. The gnawing pit in my soul was gone.

At age thirteen, my solution arrived in a perfect glass bottle with 151 written on it. My friend brought a bottle of Bacardi 151 to school. We stuck it in a vacant locker to which only a small group of us had the combination. After each class, we would meet at the locker and drink from the bottle. Magic!

That first sip changed my world. When the alcohol hit my bloodstream, it felt so good. The sensation was like a warm feeling of safety, as if a big comfortable blanket had been wrapped all around me. The Bacardi flowed down my throat, making me instantly dizzy and happy.

The lonely girl, afraid of everything and everyone, was gone. The feeling I had been dreaming of had arrived and it was spectacular. Finally, I could live life.

Even better, I didn't care what anyone thought about me. Shame vanished. Insecurity disappeared.

My friends who drank with me that day got sick. Some were caught and suspended from school. Not me. I was numb, cool and collected, and excited for more.

Instantly, my drinking became excessive—a far different experience than that of my friends.

Alcohol gave me a false sense of freedom, strength, and courage. Alcohol helped me survive and excel . . . or at least that is what I told myself to justify drinking for so many years.

Little did I know the "solution" would bring pain and suffering to my life to the point that I wanted to kill myself—and almost succeeded.

Alcohol appeared to be the key to life. Trouble at school and at home became normal, but manageable. When my father told me, I was worthless and stupid, it didn't matter. No one could hurt me. I was free.

No longer accepting my home life, I fought back, spoke up, numbed out. Soon, I realized it did not matter anyway, for no one noticed if I came home from school or was there for dinner. Instead of coming together as a family, we drifted apart.

At age fourteen, I ran away. I don't remember why, but I do remember my mother had slapped me across the face. The feeling was heartbreaking, because she was my foundation and I loved her so much. It took a lot for her to get mad, so when she did, guilt rushed through me. How could I be so bad that she was forced to hit me? Somehow, I reasoned this meant she didn't want me.

I ran away to my friend's home. We drank and roamed the neighborhood, we were free—no one could tell us anything. That did not last long. My brother found me hiding under a pool table and made me go home.

I was scared and tired, dreading walking into the house. Expecting the worst, to my surprise my father hugged me and told me he loved me. This was rare, and uncomfortable . . . not his normal behavior.

He asked if I would stay in the house. His kindness felt strange. Of course, it did not last long. Did I have a choice to go somewhere else? The thought popped into my mind: Could I leave this house for good? But things returned to normal quickly. My mother kissed and hugged me and that was enough for me to feel better. She had a way about her that made me feel special.

A pattern developed: Instead of coming home after school, I went directly to my friend's house. We had fun drinking, laughing, and walking around the neighborhood. We were inseparable, with so much in common. At last I had friends I could relate to, for they, too, came from alcoholic homes. We connected through the pain.

Around the corner from my friend's house, lived two brothers who were mechanics. They worked on cars in front of their house. We walked by their house going to school, the store, or just fooling around. They watched us and made funny comments. I did not pay much attention to them because they were so much older than my friend and me.

One day they told us to stop and talk to them, so we went over and said hello. They were funny, seemed kind, and made us feel special. Older guys were interested in us? They wanted to be friends? The attention felt good. It was so wonderful to hear someone tell me nice things. They said I was smart and pretty. I felt drawn to what I perceived as kindness, and for a while I believed them.

We began to go to their home frequently, watching them work

on cars, laughing with them and talking. They would buy beer and we would drink with them. I thought nothing of this. This was just a good time with friends, drinking and listening to music. In my young mind, this was innocent. Besides, I was not at home and that was a relief. This went on for a few weeks. They seemed just like big brothers.

One night everything changed. The evening started out the same way: having fun, drinking, and laughing together. The older brother, who had always told me how pretty I was and who had showered me with attention, asked me to look at something in his room. He was laughing and joking, telling me he wanted to show me something he made for me. His brother was there and a few friends, so I did not think anything bad would happen. I felt safe.

"I like you," he said, when I entered his room. When he said that, his tone changed. His face that was once happy and safe, turned dark and scary. I did not recognize this side of him. Suddenly I felt scared and wanted to leave.

"I need to go home," I said.

He would not let me leave. I wanted to run, but didn't know how. He was forty-eight, I was fourteen. He had a wife and a child—what was he doing?

The room became dark and cold. I was shaking, dizzy, and freezing. He took me in his arms and started to kiss me. He made me touch him. I was terrified, knowing this was wrong, but I didn't have the power to stop him. Being completely powerless was infuriating. I had trusted this man!

My legs and arms felt heavy as he forced me to the bed. I couldn't move, couldn't get off the bed. I'd had a little to drink, but this felt different. What was happening? Had he slipped me something? I broke free from his grip and stood up, as I tried to leave the room, he quickly turned and locked the door. I stood there frozen.

He was a big, stocky man and there was no way I could get away. He zipped off his mechanic's coveralls to reveal red skimpy underwear and gold chains around his neck. He said he wore these for me because I was so special.

He told me he was all mine. He asked me if I liked his body as he moved in front of me. Did he really think this was sexy?

Why is he doing this? I thought. *Aren't we friends? Is he really trying to seduce an innocent girl? How can he think this is okay?*

He stood in front of me naked. He said, "This is what two people do when they like each other."

I held on to my jacket and said I must go.

"Tell me you like me. Tell me you want me," he growled.

I would not say a word. I was too scared to speak and he knew it.

"Don't be scared, I will be good to you," he said.

"I know you have feelings for me. You visit me and you look at me. You dress in tight pants and small t-shirts for me. I know this is what you want. I know you want to be with me. I want to be with you, too."

He grabbed me and pulled me close to kissed me. I turned my face away in disgust. He violently pushed me back on to the bed. It felt like forever as I was falling backwards. My head was spinning as I reached for the bed to try and stop the fall. He was falling on top of me. The entire time I was thinking, *this is it, I did this, I came here, I trusted he was my friend, I am so stupid for believing he was a good person. I did this, it is my fault because I wanted to drink and hang out with older guys, I did this, was lying to my parents and going to his house instead of coming home, this is all my fault.*

All I could think about was, *Why can't I just go home? I will be a better girl, I will not drink.*

The thought of what was happening was so intense I felt like I was in and out of consciousness. The truth is, I was about to be raped and could not stop him.

He landed on me as my head hit the bed hard. He was so heavy it was difficult to breathe. He was no longer trying to convince me to take part in this act, he was in charge and he was pushing me and pulling on my clothes with anger and rage. I tried to push him off and kick him but that infuriated him.

"No," I said. "No, get off me. No! No!"

But he didn't listen.

He took off my clothes as I fought to put them back on. He told me to relax as his grip got tighter. He did not have to yell or say a word his actions; his strength and anger told me I had to do what he wanted. He began to rape me, over and over. I thought he would never stop.

The whole time I was saying, "No. No!"

When he was finished, he left the room. Sick to my stomach, I searched for my clothes and quickly got dressed. I wanted to get out of there.

He came back into the room. His face filled with anger. What was he going to do now? Was he going to do it again? Was he going to hurt me? Would he kill me?

He was furious. He told me I was pathetic and made too much noise. He said his mother, who lived upstairs, heard me yelling no.

His mother knew what he did, but didn't try to stop him. She never tried to help me or reach out to me after her forty-eight-year-old son raped a fourteen-year-old girl in her home.

Finally convincing him to let me go, I walked out into a dark garage. Where had his brother gone? Where were my friends? Did they know what had happened? They seemed to have just left me. Had they known his plan? Why didn't anyone help me? As I walked through the cold dark garage, his brother came up behind me with a sick smile on his face. He walked quickly to the door in front of me.

Frightened that he would hurt me too, I scooted by him as quickly as I could. As I walked by, he rubbed against me as the older brother who had just raped me looked on with a wicked smile on his face. They were sick abusers, pretending to be my friends, earning my trust and friendship for their perverted gain.

Dizzy and nauseous, I ran home. I cried, not so much from the pain, but in anger. Why was this happening? Why was my life so dreadful? What had I ever done to deserve this abuse?

Angry at myself for not having the courage to say, "Why didn't you stop when I said NO?" I said nothing. Instead, I kept my feelings inside, feeling frightened and broken.

The night he raped me, he took away my innocence. He took away my gift that God gave me. A gift that was meant to be given in love when the time came.

Now the feelings of worthlessness, humiliation and shame intensified. A good man would never want me, for I did not deserve anything good. Convinced the whole thing was my fault, I let him get away with hurting me.

That night at home I never said a word. In fact, I held the secret until now, in this writing. For forty years the pain, guilt and the humiliation stayed buried.

Although I badly wanted to tell my mother and father that a man hurt me, I couldn't. Afraid and alone, I stayed silent, letting the pain and anger grow.

Besides, I reasoned, what could my father possible do? He was always drunk and my mother had enough pain and suffering to deal with at home.

My family harbored so many secrets to justify my father's drinking. Now I had my own secret.

Drinking was the way to forget about what happened. Soon after this, I continued to hang out with friends, laughing and having a great time, as if nothing had happened. What a great little actress.

I tried to make sense of what had happened, but without a wise adult to reach out to for help, I stayed hurt, confused, and angry.

I wondered, too, was this normal? Did he like me? When would I see him again? How he would act? What would he say? Would he do it again? Would he apologize?

One day, walking by his home with my friends, we saw each other. He looked right at me, didn't say *hello* or acknowledge me in anyway. He had a new young girl on his arm, a runaway, I learned.

Devastated and humiliated, I realized he did not care about what he did to me. The pain inside was extreme. My insides sank. The reality of what he did came rushing through. I was nothing to this man. He had a sick sport, taking advantage of young, innocent girls. Anger, pain and sadness overwhelmed me once more. The reminder of how I felt the night he raped me came over me again. I had to get away from him.

With his cockiness and macho attitude, he finally looked at me and said, "You haven't been around, and like the song says, 'love the one you're with.'" He had his arm around the new victim. I wanted to tell her to get away, but the words would not come out of my mouth.

My anger grew, not only towards this man, but also towards my father. The desire to have someone hurt this man was intense. Why wasn't my father able to protect me? The feeling of having no one to tell, no one to count on, was too much to handle.

He was an abuser and should have been stopped, but I told no one. Leaving his home that day and never returning was my solution. On reflection, I wish I would have spoken up—maybe he could have been stopped before he hurt other innocent girls. But abusers count on that; they know it's likely a young victim will never tell. Indeed, I pushed it down and pretended nothing happened . . . and numbed myself further with alcohol.

Today I know better. My family loves me and they would have helped me. We could have stopped him. If not with my parents assistance, a policeman or a school counselor would have helped me.

My hope is that if any of you reading this book have experienced abuse, tell someone.

Free yourself from the guilt. Know it is not your fault. You are not responsible for any part of the abuse. Do not let the abuser take your self-worth.

Choose today to say, "I am not a victim and I am worthy of all good things in life." You *are* worthy and you are loved. It took most of my life to find my worth—do not destroy your life with regret.

Two years later, the guy came looking for me. He asked friends about me, and said he wanted to talk. I told my friends not to tell him anything about me, I wanted to keep him away. He searched for me and found where I was living.

I was living with my father at the time. As he approached the front door, I ran upstairs, telling my father to say I wasn't home.

My father was confused by my actions and, curiosity peaked, he opened the door to see a man close to his age asking for his daughter. My father had a brief discussion with him, then slammed the door.

My father shouted for me to come down. "Who was that man? Why is a man that age coming here to ask for you?"

"What did you say to him?" I asked.

"I told him he should be ashamed of himself, coming to the door asking for a sixteen-year-old girl."

This was my opportunity to tell my father the truth, to have this man arrested. But I could not find the words or the courage to speak up.

I lied to my father and told him he was a mechanic who fixed my car and was looking for more work. Nothing was ever mentioned again.

From my bedroom window, I secretly watched him walk away. He was dressed in nice slacks and a white dress shirt. Was he trying to impress me? All I could feel as he left was anger and contempt. Pushing it all down, I continued moving forward in life.

I wasted many years running from the pain and guilt of his abuse. This led me to accept abuse from men throughout my life, never accepting love from decent men, not believing I was good enough for anyone, especially a good man. Love terrified me. My life stayed guarded and shallow.

CHAPTER 3

MY BEAUTIFUL MOTHER

t was a typical foggy afternoon, laying on my bed alone in my room. I heard my parents arrive. I thought it was strange, because they rarely went out together, especially during the day. My father knocked on my bedroom door and asked me to come into the kitchen. He said he wanted to talk to me. I was confused by his tone. It was different. He was not drunk or mad; he sounded troubled. As I walked down the hall into the kitchen, I thought, *what did I do? Did they find out what happened to me?* I had no idea my life was about to change and would never be the same.

My mother was forty-eight years old. I was fifteen the day I sat down with my parents to talk . . . nervous and trying to think of an excuse for whatever I was in trouble for now.

Father said quietly, "Your mom and I went to the doctor today, and we received bad news."

My heart sank. I thought for sure my father was ill. A part of me always expected that to happen to him because of the way he drank and smoked.

But the words that came from my father's mouth weren't what I expected. I sat there in shock and disbelief when I heard him say, "Your mother is sick. She has breast cancer and needs surgery immediately."

I looked at my mother. She smiled and told me she would be fine. I'm sure she was terrified, but did not want to scare me. I was in shock and did not want to hear anymore.

I did not know how to react or what to say. All that came out of my mouth was, "You will be fine, just fine. Everything will be okay." I meant that with all my heart, for I refused to think of losing her. Denial was my solution.

The following week, my mother had surgery, and was home in bed recuperating. We tried to help and stay positive for her, but it was difficult to watch her suffer. She was so sweet—she spread love and kindness to everyone she met. She was one of those special people who made you feel better about yourself.

Why was this happening to my mom? At the age of fifteen I had already been through so much pain and suffering.

But this was by far the worst pain of all, for I could not help my mother. No one could. She was going to die and leave her family, the family she'd fought so hard to keep together.

In later years, I often wondered if the lifestyle, the tremendous amount of stress and worry she was under, caused her to get sick. I felt guilty that I was not a better daughter. I know I created stress and frustration for her, instead of bringing the peace and happiness she deserved.

But in that moment of time, I hoped my father would change, that he would stop drinking. It was his turn to help my mother. Did he have the capability to help her?

As my mother lay in bed alone, I was so full of pain and sadness for her. She had such a tough time, but she was a strong woman and fought with all her strength.

My father would not sleep in bed with her. I was angry and confused. Why, when my mother needed him the most, was he not there for her? Was it because she lost her breast? Did he not love her any longer because of that?

One day I exploded. "How can you be so cruel? Mom needs you now, more than ever. She has always been there for you, taking care of you, protecting you, and covering up when you are drunk. Why can't you take care of her and make her better?" All the pain and fear I felt just came out. He was shocked.

Alcoholics know how to take from others, but when they are needed, many cannot give the help loved ones need. My father was filled with fear and pain. Drinking was his way of checking out. My mother was his rock. He was just as scared as everyone else in the family. We were all terrified of losing her.

My father looked at me with tears in his eyes and said, "I just want your mother to be comfortable. I do not want to bother her." I realized he loved her; he was lost and trying to do his best.

As my mother lay in bed day after day, I would pretend everything was okay.

I'd lie down next to her. We'd laugh, watch TV, and talk. I loved her so much. We always had a good time together. She was funny and loved to laugh. I never talked to her about dying, and she never said a word about it to me. We just enjoyed our time together.

One day, just like any other normal day, I came home from school and went to see her. We were going over school papers. I had progress reports to be signed, and they were not good.

Usually she would sign them, tell me to do better, and never show my father.

That day was different. She told me, "It's time for you to get to know your father." I did not have a relationship with him and did not want one. I begged my mother to sign my reports, but she refused. I was so selfish, with my mother lying in bed and here I was, thinking about myself. I saw no use in telling my father, because I thought she would recover and we would just continue our little arrangement.

When she continued to refuse, I was forced to sit down with my father and show him my terrible progress reports. I thought, *here we go.* When he drank and there was an issue, he would go on for hours with his lecturing. At times, I thought to myself, *Please, just hit me and get this over with!*

This time he was different. He was supportive and kind. He told me I could do better and to try harder. I said I would and left quickly after he signed my reports, happy to get away from that conversation.

Today I know why he was so kind. He knew I was going to lose my mother and he was losing his wife, his love. He did not know how to deal with the pain. He'd been raised by an alcoholic himself and in the process, had learned not to show his true feelings, just as I had. But the feelings of loss and regret were too much for him to bear. He drank excessively and tried to bury the pain, but when the alcohol quit working he was in turmoil.

Mother's health was not getting better. She asked to go to the hospital, not wanting to pass at home. She knew her life was ending.

The hospital was far away, and it was difficult for me to get there because I was too young to drive. I wanted to be with her. Many days I did not go to school and went straight to the hospital instead. On the days I went to school, I rushed out of class right after the bell rang.

I quickly ran to the bus stop for an hour-long ride to reach the city where the hospital was located. After the bus ride, I walked another thirty minutes to the hospital. I did this daily to be with her. We were happy to see each other. Somedays she told me I smelled like smoke. I had started to smoke cigarettes when I drank. I just looked at her with a shy smile. We knew there was little time left together, so we did not talk about it. I knew she did not approve.

I wanted this all to be a dream, one where I would wake up and she would be healthy.

Mother fought hard, but eventually lost her battle to cancer. She died within eight months of her diagnosis. During her illness, I witnessed her strength and her love for her family. All she wanted was for all of us to be happy and stay together.

The last day of her life, she was having a rough time, suffering so much.

My brothers and sisters and I were gathered around her hospital bed. The doctors told us she had very little time. She was trying to hang on, waiting for my father. Where was he? No one knew.

Finally, we heard his heels clicking down the hospital hallway, the characteristic sound of the silver taps on the heels of his boots. She must have heard him too, because she perked up. She stared at the doorway, waiting for him to come into view. They loved each other so much, but their love story was ending. The good life my father promised her was just a distant memory now. Most of their time together was spent in the turmoil of addiction, broken dreams, and lonely nights.

As I stood there watching her pass away, I wished we could all go back in time, that somehow, we could live a peaceful and healthy life, a life filled with happiness and love, not chaos and sadness. I was despondent watching her lie in bed, fighting for breath.

Her life was ending far too soon.

I realized I would never share happy times with her again. I would miss her touch, her soft skin, and her gentle way of letting me know everything would be okay, even when she knew it would not be.

I would miss our Sunday mornings lying in bed, reading the comics together. The little things that I often took for granted or brushed aside.

Suddenly, I wished I would not have started drinking and had spent more time at home. All the bad things I did rushed through my mind. I would never have the chance to make it up to her. She was leaving this world. I was not the daughter I wanted to be, and felt she deserved better.

As she lay dying in the hospital room, that part of me that she filled with her pure, honest love died with her. I could never replace my mother's love for me. I knew the life ahead of me would be filled with a deep hole in my soul.

My father hated hospitals. He rarely visited while she was ill, but now he had to be here, he had to say goodbye to his wife, friend, and mother of his five children.

When he walked into the room, heartbreak was written all over his face. He kept his strength, his courage, and his composure. I was proud of my father at that moment. I saw that he could be a good man, a strong man.

He took my mother's hand and said, "Mary. We are all here. It's okay. You are okay." It was as if he gave her permission to let go. She looked relieved. She was always the strong one, even though she did not look it. She was a little, blonde, blue-eyed, beautiful woman, but she had a solid strength inside. She needed that strength to take care of five children and an alcoholic husband. Now she was free; she did not have to be strong any longer.

As she struggled to breathe, she called for her father who had passed away a few years before. I thought this was strange, but later learned that some believe when you are ready to cross over your loved ones who have passed on come to help in your journey.

Her breathing calmed, she ceased struggling, and her face, once full of pain and fear, was now relaxed. She even had a small smile on her face.

Mother took her last breath and left this world in peace, surrounded by her children and husband. She was loved and we all sent our love and prayers with her. I am so grateful I was granted the honor to watch her cross over with love and contentment on her face. The feeling that she was at peace helped me go through the pain of losing her.

Sitting in the hospital room after my mother passed, I thought, *who is going to take care of me now?* On my way home, it hit me: *I am stuck living with my alcoholic father, without the love and protection of my mother.* Walking out of the hospital that night, I was numb. I continued to live my life in that state for many years.

In the middle of the night, three nights after she died, I was awakened. I opened my eyes to see my mother sitting on my bed, wearing a robe I had given her when she was sick. She looked at me with her sweet smile and I felt her love; I saw her peace and knew she would always be with me. I know she has been in my life guiding me through my darkest days ever since. I feel her presence and pray that one day, I will make her proud of me.

After my mother died, my father's drinking became unstoppable. He drank all day, every day. He was in so much pain. The loss was devastating for all of us. He lost his love, his wife. He also was dealing with the guilt of all the years of drinking and putting my mother through so much pain and misery. He told me it was difficult to forget the way he treated her.

Our family was distraught, even more broken than before. Each dealt with the pain of our mother's death in our own way. We had no counseling. We barely talked to each other. We just went on and buried the pain.

I do not remember crying when she died. The only emotion I felt was anger.

All I could think was, *why is my life so painful? What did I do wrong? Why did I have to go through this? Why did she leave me?* I was focused on my life, rather then what my mother left behind.

The day came when we had to clean out our mother's things from her bedroom. My father lay sprawled on the bed, drunk, telling us not to touch her things. But we knew we had to pack them away. Sorting through her belongings was agonizing. She was a humble woman who never wanted much. Most of her belongings consisted of costume jewelry and inexpensive clothes—but they were perfect. She always shined. And everyone had been drawn to her light.

We packed up her clothes to donate to our church. We felt this was a good thing to do, that the church would give the clothes to poor families in need.

My father forced us to go to church every Sunday, but he didn't go. I thought it was such a joke since he was the one who needed church, not us. Some days my brother and I would take money that he gave us for the basket, skip church and buy candy. Those were my favorite Sundays.

Not long after we donated her clothes, we went to church. That Sunday, a nun walked by, wearing my mother's dress, the dress my sisters and I had given her on her birthday. I was appalled. How could she wear our mother's clothes, knowing she had recently passed away and her mourning children would be at mass?

I was livid and I used that anger to justify never going to church or thinking of God again. The only time I thought of God was when I was in trouble. Then I prayed. I did not feel God in my life. I thought I was not worthy of God's love and did not care. Today I know that God was always there, waiting for me to let him into my life.

Living with my father was difficult. I watched him trying to drink himself to death. My brothers and sisters were living on their own by then. They asked me to leave my father and live with them. At times, I wanted to leave, but I remembered what my mother told me when I was ten years old. *Your father is sick and we need to take care of him.*

I stayed, trying to help him.

As time went on, and his drinking became worse, all I could think was, I am going to lose my father soon, too. He will die from alcoholism.

He would somehow buy alcohol every day. I found it hidden around the house.

I drank some, poured some out, and replaced it with water. He was so polluted with alcohol he didn't know the difference.

He spent his days drinking at the neighborhood bar, then in the evening he'd call for a ride home. I would pick him up. All the way home he would curse me, tell me I was a bitch and a whore. I knew he was a drunk, so I did not say a word or feel a thing. This was my life. I was just moving forward, not feeling, just going through the motions.

He looked terrible and I knew he would pass away if he did not stop drinking. He would not eat or shower. He laid in bed in so much agony. I related to his pain, because I knew what he was feeling long before my addiction brought me to the same demoralizing place in life.

Addiction is a deadly disease, but people do not look at it that way. Instead, they judge. My aunts and uncles said he was a useless drunk, that he would be better off dead. I saw something different; I knew there was a good man underneath the disease.

Many times, I called the ambulance, but he would refuse help. He was stubborn and defiant and I began to lose hope. No matter how much my father drank or how badly he treated me, he was my father and I loved him. I did not want to lose him, too. I was miserable in the middle of this chaos.

Finally, after many days without food or water, he fell. His body simply gave out. He hit his head on the kitchen floor, drunk, bleeding, and close to death. I was terrified.

Standing over him in a panic, I asked, "Dad are you done?

He said, "Yes."

Yes, he finally said *yes!*

He agreed to be admitted to a hospital. As I sat outside his hospital room, watching as he was tied down to the bed and then went through the agony of detox, it was scary to witness. Never did I imagine that one day I would be in the exact same position, fighting for my life.

My father never drank again. Finally, I saw his true nature. My father was a better man than I could have ever wished for. We became close, and through the hard times we formed a strong bond that kept us together. He taught me many things in life—he especially taught me that I should never give up. I am proud to say he became my best friend, through good times and bad times. When my heart was broken by a boy, I sat in his lap and cried, just like I wanted to do when I was a little girl.

What a blessing we can be to others when alcohol is removed from our lives.

CHAPTER 4

PARTY TIME

My father was doing well without alcohol, so home life began to settle down. It was time to think about my life. What did I want to do and how to begin? My past continued to haunt me, for thinking about what happened caused a constant battle in my mind. Still blaming and torturing myself, coupled with the pain of missing my mother, I didn't feel able to move forward without drinking. I did not want to think about the past and did not reach out for help—instead I chose to drink and party to forget.

A friend introduced me to cocaine. I liked it and could drink more when I used it, but my true desire was alcohol. I could handle alcohol . . . drugs made me feel out of control. Looking back, alcohol controlled my life from the first sip. While abusing alcohol, my thoughts were distorted. For example, I was angry with my mother. How could she leave me? Instead of feeling pain, the only emotion I was familiar with was anger. I used this anger for many years and hid behind the pain while drinking and living it up.

My family began to move on and put their lives together. I could not seem to do the same. Somehow, I managed to graduate from high school. I enrolled in college with the thought of becoming a prosecuting attorney to help change the world and punish criminals.

Studying law was tough. I had so much homework, papers due, and lectures. It was a heavy load, made heavier because drinking and partying was the priority. My friends had good jobs and drank every night after work. As I watched everyone around me having a good time, I wanted an easy life for myself—or at least that was my excuse. The truth is, I did not think I was smart enough, nor believe I could be anyone important. Frightened to do anything outside my comfort zone, I made excuses.

My father was starting a company, so I decided to take a semester off school *to help him out.* That was my rationalization. Now I could work and drink with no books, tests, or teachers looming over me.

Nightly, my friends and I would stay up partying until five in the morning, then get up and go to work, swearing we would not drink again. Yet at five-thirty that same day, we would make our way to the local bar. We were not even at the legal age to drink, but we had fake identification. Mine said I was thirty-two: I looked fifteen. The bartenders would laugh and say, "What would you like?" Music to my ears!

No one seemed to care. As long we were good customers and did not cause trouble, we were admitted to any bar.

We often drank in San Francisco, where we hopped from bar to bar. St. Patrick's Day was a favorite. Everyone was drunk and crazy. My friends and I drove home many nights completely intoxicated. Thank God, we never killed ourselves or anyone else. We did run over a guy's foot once as he was trying to get in our car. We were six drunk girls, and he was bothering us.

"Hit the gas!" we yelled at the driver, and she ran over his foot. We dissolved into laughter. "Hey, man, that wasn't cool!" he yelled. We figured he was okay, and drove off, laughing all the way to another bar. Later that evening, we ran into him again and laughed and drank with him.

Things like that happened all the time. Instead of worrying that we could have hurt someone or that we were taking things too far, maybe even considering that we needed to slow down, we just kept going. We thought we were having the time of our lives. On one hand, we had so much fun, but on the other, we were mean, uncaring and living dangerously.

Once, friends and I drank all night in San Francisco, then boredom struck.

"Let's go skiing," someone suggested. We jumped in the car and drove, intoxicated, to Lake Tahoe, travelling through the mountains in the middle of the night, just four drunk girls. We never thought about the risk of driving in mountains in the winter. We were on a mission to party.

We arrived at the resort before opening, met the ski patrol in the lodge, and the party began. They had been up all night too, some in worse shape than us. Wherever we went, we found a party. We never thought about sleep or eating a good meal, all we wanted was to drink and have fun. We pushed ourselves to the limit.

That weekend, we did not drive home on Sunday evening. We were too busy drinking. Monday morning was difficult: we piled in the car for the long drive home, tired, still intoxicated, and swearing we would never do it again, all the while laughing about all the fun we'd had.

Our first stop was San Francisco, where my friend's father owned a restaurant. She was the manager. Normally she arrived early to set up the dining room. This was an upscale restaurant in the financial district of San Francisco. Clientele were lawyers, judges and professional business people.

We drove up to the front of the restaurant, all of us in bad shape, reeking of alcohol. My friend was still dressed in skiing attire and carrying skis and boots.

Her father met her at the door and was horrified to see she was in such a disheveled state. He looked at us in complete distain. The lunch crowd was already waiting for service and knew her well. They, too, looked at her in disbelief.

To us in the car, this was priceless. We laughed so hard, honking the horn and screaming out to her. Her father just shook his head. He knew us and was used to our stupidity. But at that moment he was not pleased; we had no regard for him or his business.

We had many good times but we also had many heartaches. The girl we dropped off at her father's restaurant had a breakdown and was sick for months with delusional thoughts and paranoia. She had attended a party where she was given tainted drugs. She has since recovered, but it was a scary time for her and for all of us who loved her.

We had close friends killed in car and motorcycle accidents because of alcohol. Our lives were surrounded by the chaos of addiction. We were running fast through life, never planning, with no dreams of getting married and settling down. Most girls dream about a wedding and babies. Not us. We just went for it, never thinking about any ramifications from our partying. We thought everyone lived this way in their twenties.

I was having way too much fun drinking and didn't want a guy to slow me down. Treating guys terribly, using and discarding them, I didn't know how to love. In fact, I had no interest in love. Numb and intoxicated, running around without a care in the world made me feel safe and in control.

When I did not drink, I felt alone, unhappy, and hurt. I kept that part of me hidden from the world. I only showed the strong, funny girl who had it all together. On the outside, I was perfect: dressed nicely, in good shape, surrounded by money and material possessions. Inside I felt broken.

As time went on, my brothers and sisters were all married or in long-term relationships. I thought maybe getting married would make me feel better. Perhaps, I reasoned, my unhappiness was because I was single. Once again, I was caught in the pattern of always looking for something outside myself for happiness.

CHAPTER 5

MARRIAGE AND BABIES

Drinking every night at the bars and running around town started to get to me. Only in my early twenties, I had already been drinking heavily for seven years. It was time to settle down and start a family . . . or at least that occurred to be the solution to my drinking.

Briefly, I became engaged, but the relationship was filled with alcohol and drugs. We had a brutal break up and never spoke again.

My drinking friends had begun to settle down. Some were married with children. I thought they looked happy and content. I wanted to be happy with a good man and get married too. My problem was, I knew nothing about marriage or how to even recognize a good man.

Dating was not my expertise: I picked damaged, good-looking, reckless men. The relationships were short and full of drama. Perfect, during my wild drinking times, but I was different now, I told myself.

Now, how to find a good man? This was my new obsession. Every time I had something in my mind, I had to conquer it, not letting it rest until I succeeded in getting whatever person, place or thing I wanted. A husband was no different.

One day I had lunch with a girlfriend, who was recently married and had a new baby.

We sat in a nice restaurant, discussing ways to find a good man, then, just like that, the quest ended. My husband-to-be walked by our table.

He was my brother's friend and a waiter at the restaurant. We knew each other from high school. He was older, handsome, and charismatic.

This was my guy. He would be my husband; I felt certain and did everything in my power to make him marry me.

After six months of dating, he asked me to marry him. During the time we dated, I pretended I would be the perfect wife. I didn't know how to do anything domestic. I did not cook or know how to prepare meals, so I paid my girlfriend to cook our meals. She was an excellent chef. After work, I would rush to her house and pick up the finished meals, packing them in my car as my friend and her husband looked on and laughed. They asked me, how are you going to keep up this charade for thirty years? I never gave that a second thought.

I arrived home before my fiancé got off work. I set the table and placed the perfectly cooked meals in our dishes. When he walked in the house, I proudly told him, "I made your favorite dinner tonight honey."

He was good looking, honest, and hardworking: the perfect man . . . except for one small detail. He was an alcoholic who had just finished his second stint in rehab when we met. *Well,* I thought, *perfect. He doesn't drink, so I won't.*

We lived together before the wedding, immediately sensing something was not right. I had the desire to leave, feeling I must get out of there, but I told myself I would feel different when we married. Why did I feel lonely and unhappy still?

Life without alcohol was too boring and I began to grow restless, so I started to drink two glasses of wine each night. Big glasses. I made sure to buy big wine goblets.

When my friends came to visit, they would laugh about the size of my wine glasses. I could drink a bottle of wine in two glasses. Alcoholics are smart. We are very creative in our disease. A bottle a night was good for now!

Planning the wedding became an excuse to party. There were so many opportunities to go out drinking with my girlfriends. We had a blast. I kept telling myself, *I will quit drinking when I get married. Until then, I am living it up.*

My friends began to ask, "Does it bother you that your fiancé can't drink? Are you sure you want to be with a man who cannot drink?" They all knew me as a happy-go-lucky party girl, but I told myself I could be different.

My friends married men that drank. They continued to have fun and party with their husbands. I was going into my marriage thinking marriage would settle me down and I'd become the perfect mother and wonderful wife. Besides, he didn't seem to mind if I had my two big glasses of wine each night. I just assumed he was fine with it.

The morning of my wedding day was beautiful. Surrounded by family and friends, with my closest friends in the wedding party, it was perfect. Drinking champagne, laughing, not thinking about getting married, it seemed like a big party and I was feeling good. Until the ceremony began.

As my father walked me down the aisle, he slowed down and said to me, "Honey, I do not care how much money I spent on this wedding. If you do not want to go through with this marriage, we can turn around right now. I will take care of everything. Shocked, I wondered why was he saying this to me now. Was it because he saw me and my friends drinking bottles of champagne before the wedding? I didn't know what to say.

I assured him this was the right thing for me, so we walked in silence the rest of the way to the alter. My father knew me well. He loved me so much and he loved my soon-to-be husband. But he knew I was just like him; he raised me to think, feel and act just like him. He knew quitting drinking was not easy, but he could not help me. Instead, he just loved me.

Walking down the aisle, I was unaware of the baggage I was carrying with me: the unresolved pain and suffering, the addiction I would not acknowledge. This dysfunction followed me into my new life. I was good at hiding, but now I had nowhere to hide, nowhere to isolate when things were difficult. I was sharing my life, my home, and my space with someone.

Living with my husband, my flaws quickly became apparent to me and to him. My deepest fears were magnified, staring me in my face. I was forced to acknowledge them, but I did not know how to deal with them. All I knew was how to blame, judge, and criticize. Our marriage was full of loneliness and distance.

We played the game well; we knew how to pretend we were fine. We were cordial to each other and truly good friends. The chemistry between the two of us was missing however. We did not behave like two young newlyweds should. Or was I comparing our love to my reckless relationships of the past? Drinking and meeting men, I was not as inhibited as I was in my marriage. My husband was recently sober, starting a new chapter in his life. We were both afraid to talk about sex. It was so confusing. We avoided each other at night; he stayed up late watching television, I went to sleep early, to begin each day at 5:00 a.m.

We both had many insecurities. He was an alcoholic, who wasn't drinking, but not living in the solution, he was miserable. I was an alcoholic who was still drinking and not realizing my addiction. We did not know how to deal with our pasts, because we were both buried in pain and denial. We took it out on each other. Two broken people, looking at each other to fix one another, we found out quickly that two broken people cannot fix anyone.

We remained married and soon had two handsome boys. We had it all. The babies, careers, house, cars, and money in the bank. Everything society says we should have to be happy. *What is wrong with him?* I thought. *Why can't he make me happy?* I never looked inside for answers. It was so much easier to blame him.

I loved my husband and my children the best way I knew how. Feelings of love, joy and peace scared me. Contentment felt unfamiliar. Chaos, dysfunction and feeling numb felt better. I knew and liked those feelings. This was not me.

When my boys were babies, I watched my husband hug and kiss them. I did not know how to do that with my children. Affection felt uncomfortable. I was distant with my love—guarded and scared to death. Unfortunately, even with my children.

Not totally realizing I was denying my boys love, but being blocked in that regard, I disguised my behavior through being busy.

This helped me keep my distance from everyone and I could justify my behavior by telling myself I was important, I was supporting the household. I convinced myself that working hard and earning money was doing the right thing by my sons. Today, I know that love, time, and affection are all children crave from a parent.

The feelings of loneliness and unhappiness began to get to me. Chaos, craziness, and passion—either good or bad—were missing from my life.

Our marriage was ending and it was heartbreaking. Our sons witnessed our yelling and screaming, and of course blamed themselves for our divorce. My oldest asked me if it was because of him that we did not love each other any longer. This broke my heart. I wanted the marriage to work; I wanted a happy family for my children. So far removed from our relationship, I did not know how to turn things around to salvage our marriage.

Even for the sake of my sons, I could not see away to make things better. We held on to the bitter end, we blamed one another, lied, cheated, and then I ran. I knew how to be selfish and leave relationships, but this time it was different. I was destroying my sons' lives too. I hated myself for hurting my children. Throughout their childhood I spoiled them with material possessions, vacations, and money to make up for my behavior. I never wanted to hurt them, but I did. The guilt follows me to this day.

After our divorce, my ex-husband began to drink excessively. I tried hard to help him stop drinking, wanting him to be a good father to our boys. My life was full of chaos. I was raising my boys, running a company, and trying to keep my ex-husband sober. While some people would have collapsed, I thrived in the madness. This is where I felt the best. The distractions kept my mind occupied and off my issues.

My friends and family would ask, "How do you do it? You are so strong."

I was not strong. I ran on fear and didn't look at my life or my drinking. I deflected my struggles by trying to fix everything and everyone around me—except me.

CHAPTER 6

THE TUMBLE BEGINS

s my first marriage was ending, I met another man. This compli-
cated life even more, but also provided happiness and affection
that I had been craving. I believed he was the man of my dreams.
Handsome and adventurous, he showered me with passion, gifts,
flowers, romantic cards and dinners. He had two children also: a boy
and a girl. Our children loved each other, and it seemed we had the
perfect extended family. Together we made magic.

He came from a wonderful family, full of love and kindness. His
mother and father were loving and caring parents. Instantly I became
extremely close to his sisters and brothers. We shared many wonderful
times together. His family loved me and my sons, they welcomed us into
their hearts and homes, and we experienced pure love and joy every time
we were together. My sons loved the delicious food and music that was
part of the family parties.

Watching my son's hearts filled with joy and happiness was such a pleasure. I thought *finally they see true love in a family.* I soon discovered that everything was not so perfect. This great love blinded me from the many red flags in the beginning of our relationship. Starving for love and belonging, I turned my head to this man's controlling and dishonest behavior.

He loved smoking marijuana; he was high most of the day. When he was not high he was angry or asleep. I loved my wine, he loved his marijuana. Everything was perfect, I reasoned, thinking this was so much better than being with an alcoholic. His smoking allowed me the freedom to drink excessively without feeling irresponsible. If he ever said a word about my drinking, I would attack his smoking.

We had many fun times with the children but I was always thinking inside, when and how can I leave this relationship? I stayed way too long for all the wrong reasons.

After living together and fighting for years, we finally made our dysfunction legitimate. He planned a romantic night out in beautiful San Francisco, with a limo ride, roses, and dinner at my favorite restaurant, The Starlight Room. We were drinking, laughing and dancing. When the two of us were together we had a wonderful time and sparks flew. I had hope that this time we could be different, but the beautiful nights always ended in mayhem. We were reckless together, we drank too much, then the violent fights would begin.

This night was no different, but before we started to argue, he got down on one knee and proposed. I was intoxicated, feeling so special, so of course I said yes. Our relationship was explosive: good passion and bad abuse. We never knew what way the evening would end.

Many times, I blacked out and woke up the next day in a panic, trying to put the pieces together.

That night, even though I was intoxicated and feeling like a princess as he showered me with love and affection, my instincts were screaming, run, *this will not end well.* I felt danger, but continued to drink to quiet the feelings. I did not know how to stand up for myself and say *no.*

The next morning, I was not excited to be engaged, I was embarrassed. Knowing how he treated me and others was killing me inside. I knew better, so why was I staying with him? Again, my thinking was, *I will take care of everything, we will be happy.*

My family, friends, a few of his close friends, even my ex-husband told me to get away from him. They all warned me not to go through with the wedding. They were right, but I could not leave him. He knew exactly what to do and say to keep me down. He robbed me of my self-worth. Feeling stuck, physically and mentally, I gave up on myself. It was painful to feel so humiliated. Why couldn't I walk away? I was broken inside but still carried myself like a strong and confident woman.

He formed a close bond with my younger son. My older son did not accept him and kept his distance, but eventually bonded with him. He used the love he had with my sons against me whenever he wanted anything. He had to have the best—travel to exotic beaches, expensive cars, boats, motorcycles—anything that was new and exciting we bought.

He would use the children, saying, "think of all the fun they will have", as he poured me another glass of chardonnay, knowing I would give in and pay for everything after a few glasses.

We traveled to picturesque places, always bringing along his friend. He needed help with equipment was the excuse, but the reality was he wanted a friend to smoke and party with. I was often left alone with the kids. I loved being with the children, but the resentment and anger grew. He had all the fun and freedom while I worked hard every day.

The stress of maintaining this lifestyle lay on my shoulders, as I worked hard to make the income needed to sustain our reckless spending. I was always trying to keep up with his expensive desires.

And it wasn't just the travel. He would tear half the house apart and not finish the construction until I paid more for labor. I was handing him envelopes full of cash to pay the workers each Friday. To my horror I found out after our remodel was completed that he was taking half the cash for himself and not paying the crew. I knew these men. I trusted and respected them. When I found out what he did to them, I was furious and humiliated.

Each day when the crew arrived to work, I spoke with them. I had plenty of food and drinks available and made sure they had enough supplies, anything they needed to feel comfortable in our home.

They worked hard for us.

I did not know he was not paying them in full. I must have looked so disingenuous.

The men never said a word to me about the money. When I found out what was going on, I asked them why they had not told me. They said, out of respect they did not want to hurt me or ruin my marriage.

Instead, they showed up each day, working hard to finish the job with hopes of being paid in full at completion. That is what my husband promised them. These men worked extremely hard and had families to feed. My husband willfully stole their wages for his own benefit and lied to me about the money.

He had so many dreams and plans, he would ask me weekly to fund his latest millionaire invention. I would say *no,* and the silent treatment, sleeping on the couch and throwing out insults would begin. He was never steady with financial support.

He owed money to many vendors. When he did not pay, they came looking for me. This was humiliating. My self-respect, never strong, was gone completely and now my perfect credit and the money I worked so hard for all my life was being depleted.

Drowning myself in alcohol to cope with the extreme financial stress, my drinking was out of control. The arguments were daily, finances and respect were the topic of evening battles. When I brought up the subject of money, he flipped.

He turned every argument into something I did wrong, laying all the blame on me. By the end of the discussion I was the culprit. The horrifying thing is, I believed him. He was a master at manipulation.

Discovering his dark side was painful and demoralizing. He was a thief and a liar, stealing from me and others. Even though I hated this, I could not find the strength or courage to get out of the marriage. Feeling guilty for leaving my first husband, I did not want to fail at this marriage, too. Again, I pretended everything was fine. Frightened and alone, I was in trouble.

The abuse in our relationship began early on, it started with verbal abuse, on both sides. I was not innocent when it came to the verbal abuse. When the physical abuse began, I was shocked and terrified.

The first time he hit me, I had been out to dinner with my boys. He was always jealous if he was left out. I enjoyed my time with my children, having the chance to just connect, the three of us. We needed time together alone in peace. I worked on the other side of the bay, where my children went to school. I'd pick the boys up after work and take them to dinner. We avoided rush hour traffic and had time to relax together.

I came into the house one evening after a nice dinner with the boys. My husband was pouting about missing dinner with us. I knew the only thing he was upset about was missing a good dinner and free drinks.

The arguments began. I was exhausted, this was nightly, same fight every night, so I decided to take a hot bath. As I lay in the bath, the argument intensified. He rushed into the bathroom and grabbed and choked me. I was petrified and unable to stop him. He pushed my head under the bath water and held me down. It seemed like eternity. I thought my life was over.

He finally released me, with pure hatred on his face, he said, "That is what you get, and there is more to come." He was right, there was a lot more to come.

I was in shock, hating him more than I had ever hated anyone in my life, besides myself. How could I allow this to happen? I told myself, *I am a strong intelligent woman allowing this man to almost kill me in my home, in front of my children.* My son heard the commotion and came running to help me. *This is it, I am leaving him immediately,* I promised myself.

I talked to my children, trying to make sense of his behavior to them and to myself and went to bed that night with the intention of packing up and moving out. My children deserved a better life. I locked our bedroom doors and went to sleep.

The next day I woke up and remembered what happened. Ashamed, I absorbed the blame. He told me it was my fault because my drinking and verbal abuse caused him to explode.

Embarrassed about my drinking and my anger; I thought if I spoke better to him we would not fight. I convinced myself that I deserved being abused physically, emotionally and financially.

This was the beginning of being physically abused by the man I thought once had saved my life from a lonely and unhappy marriage. I would have given anything to be married to my first husband again. Sometimes we do not see the goodness right in front of our eyes.

My entire life, I was so afraid of being alone, leaping from one relationship to the other. I could not stand the thought of living alone. Time and time again, I begged him not to leave me. This was by far the most humiliating part of the cycle of abuse. This would feed his ego and give him power he was lacking in his own self-worth. He constantly told me I was a horrible mother and wife and he was my victim. He knew the buttons to push. I believed him. I felt insane, and he knew it. I did not want anyone to know the crazy side of me; I was still pretending life was great and I was fine.

I accepted his behavior and the physical abuse that was more and more frequent. He knew how to hurt me and scare me with the threat of abandonment.

Another night, driving home from a party in San Francisco, we had both been drinking, and the arguing began. Exhausted, I did not want to fight, but again, I was not one to keep my mouth shut.

We were driving through Oakland after midnight, He grabbed my head and bashed it into the console of his truck. I was half asleep, thinking *what is going on?*

He was furious, yelling and screaming, telling me to get out of the truck. I was begging him *no,* just as he knew I would. He loved the power the abuse gave him. He knew this was his way to control me.

I was humiliated, wanting desperately to jump out of the truck and get away from him for good. Thoughts of dying went through my mind. Hoping if I died he would suffer with remorse the rest of his life. Realizing that jumping from the truck would kill me or severely injure me, I sat still. Thinking of my boys, I wanted another chance to be a good mother to them.

I did not want to die and leave my sons. So again, I took the abuse, buried the pain and humiliation. I was finding a way to live this abusive lifestyle instead of getting out, I was accepting my fate.

This was not the last time I suffered such abuse. I hated him, but thought I needed him.

My drinking was out of control. He knew it and made sure I stayed defeated. If I showed signs of strength, he always found a way to bring me back down. I was losing this battle. I was so concerned with what others thought about me, I chose to let this man abuse me and destroy my spirit. It was a sick and painful way to live.

I called the police a few times and had him arrested, but did not press charges, instead staying with him out of fear. His rage against me was fueled by jealousy. "You talk too much! You're too friendly," he'd say. He wanted me to give him all my attention.

Dinner one night at our favorite restaurant turned quickly into a night of terror. He flew into a jealous rage when the waiter kissed me on the cheek. The waiter was a young man from Italy. My husband knew him well; he waited on us and the children frequently. I never knew what would upset my husband. But when I drank, I did not care and the fights would begin.

Leaving the restaurant, he yelled and screamed at me, shouting that I was a slut and wanted to be with the waiter. Angry and degraded, but terrified he would abuse me, I stayed away from him that evening when we arrived home. I went to sleep, hoping he would not hit me. When the children were with us he played the good father and loving husband. He was smart and dangerous.

The next day he left for a surf trip, or off to have another affair. At the time, I was so naïve about what was truly going on in our relationship and didn't find out until after our divorce about all the women he had been with, bringing them into my home behind my back or taking them with him on excursions at my expense.

I was so upset when I woke up, I had to have a drink to settle my nerves and get to work. That was an excuse to drink, of course, but I was miserable, thinking I had no way out. He treated me like this and now he was on a great surf trip. My anger at him and myself was so debilitating I drank just to function.

That day I remember feeling fine after drinking my vodka. I was off to the office. I woke up, lying in a hospital emergency room. I crashed my SUV into a tree. Was I trying to kill myself? To this day, I do not remember anything.

In the hospital, I overheard the nurses talking about me, calling me "the woman who was drunk at eight in the morning." I felt so low, so humiliated. I did not want to be this woman. I wanted to feel good, healthy, happy. *What happened to my life? How did I get here? Why is this happening to me?* So many times, in my life I asked myself those questions, but never took the time to look inside, to see what changes I could make to create a better life for me and my sons.

The doctors asked me to call a family member to help me get home. I would not call my family. The hospital called my husband, who was out of town; his sister met me at the hospital and took me home.

My husband flew home early to take care of me, to play the hero. He loved to make himself look like the strong husband with a sick, crazy wife. I was sick and he was making me crazy. I did not have any fight left in me to tell myself or anyone the truth. I felt like I was dying, and some days it felt like the best thing for me to just pass away, out of this pain.

He kept my family away so they did not know the truth. We played this dysfunctional dance for years. It was sad, sick, and exhausting for both of us. He was getting want he wanted out of the relationship: cars, house, money and freedom to do anything he wanted. I worked and made the money and tried to be a good mother to my children and his while trying to keep up the façade of a happy woman.

I often told myself no other man would love me: my life was a mess. I drank and hid from my family, who I now know would have done anything to help me. As far as they knew, I was fine. Deep down they knew there was trouble in my life but whenever they'd ask, I assured them I was happy, just under a lot of stress.

Although I was making all the money, I worried about how to support my children financially if I left him. I could not see he was the one spending our money. I could easily take care of myself and my children. The abuse and addiction put me in survival mode. *Just get through the day,* became my mantra. I could not see a way out.

My friends and family begged me to leave him. I stayed with him out of fear, loneliness and pride. I did not want to hear *I told you so.* I risked my life and my children's life for my ego and pride. My main concern was to keep up the charade. I wasted so many years concerned about what others thought of me. I could not see that the people who truly mattered to me in my life wanted me happy, healthy and safe. They loved me, but I had to find that out the hard way.

With my drinking out of control, there was no longer any relief or fun. I became irresponsible at work, losing my ability to hold it all together. The pretense was over; my life started to crumble and I fell hard.

The lies I lived by and the stories I told myself were powerful and damaging. A man never has the right to touch a woman, no matter what. I accepted his behavior because I felt damaged.

Being abused I carried the guilt and shame with me, throughout my lifetime. I held onto to the blame which allowed me to accept abusive behavior.

Worst of all, my children witnessed much of this dysfunction. I made excuses for my behavior and my husband's. They knew better. I was wrong to not think of them first. I was repeating the pattern of my life: my children had to endure the insanity of living with two addicted parents.

If I did not have strength to leave for me, why didn't I have the strength to leave for them? This reality filled me with shame. My children, my boys. I loved them so much, yet I was sick and weak, and did not reach out for help.

That is the battle of addiction. Knowing I should not drink, but convincing myself that I could drink like I had in the past, just control the drinking more. Just one. It'll be fine. But it wasn't fine. And it was never just one.

I also convinced myself that my husband and I had once been truly in love and could be again. When he would try to win me back after hitting me, he would shower me with love and swear it would be better.

I did not want to have to admit I was being abused. I wanted the days back when we were in love, but just like with drinking, I could not go back.

I was losing my life, a little bit each day.

CHAPTER 7

THE HEARTACHE OF REGRET

A constant battle ensued daily just to function. Depressed, over-weight, drinking and in an abusive marriage, I couldn't help but wonder how long this agony would last. But what I faced each day was nothing compared to what was about to enter my life. In the middle of a rainstorm of misery, little did I know a hurricane's worth was heading for my life.

The one part of my life where I found peace, besides engaging with my children, was through my business. I'd worked with my family for over thirty years and we'd built a successful business. I knew what to do each day and thrived in a business setting despite the problems at home and with my drinking. I loved the daily challenges and the hard work that building a business demanded. All of this changed when the recession hit the Bay Area in 2007.

Our clients were homeowners, contractors and builders. In 2007 the housing market collapsed. The effect of the collapse was sudden. Overnight, business seemed to dry up. My father had retired years before, leaving my brothers and myself to run the company.

We were shocked and in a panic, struggling to know how to make it through without losing the company. Until the recession, we'd never endured difficult financial times.

Frightened, my brothers and I began to fight amongst ourselves, blaming each other for the business failing. Instead of coming together to find a solution, we pointed fingers. Struggling to keep our crews working, we cut hours, wages, we even stopped paying ourselves to pay our employees. We hung on, thinking the recession would end quickly, and business would bounce back so the thriving company could recover, but the recession lingered and it tore my brothers and I apart.

The effects of the recession were devastating to many. I watched in horror as business after business closed. Some belonged to good friends who lost everything they'd worked for all their lives. I met professors and engineers in their late sixties, forced to work at Target after losing all their retirement money in the crash.

In this dark and depressing time, I was surprised by a few people who accepted this as a lesson in life. They believed life was not possessions or money and that they could learn and grow from hardships. Their core foundation of each day was the gratitude of having their health and love of family and friends. They were hopeful and had faith in life. Seeing this, I wondered, *did I have any faith in life? Did I have faith in myself?*

I began to consider life differently. Maybe there was a way out of days filled with one disaster after the other. On top of the abusive marriage and crumbling business, the father of my children began drinking all day, isolating himself from his family and friends. I needed to be clear-headed to work my way out of this: I quit drinking. Although this was difficult, for the first time I liked being sober. Something changed inside.

I managed to quit drinking for a month. I white-knuckled it, just forcing myself not to drink, doing it for my sons. They were going through a difficult time with their dad. When he drank he was angry and took it out on the boys. They came to live with me full-time, which was not much better, but I tried to keep it together for them.

We had all been through so much. I wanted to get away, take the boys on a trip. So, we packed up the motorcycles and took off for the desert. We loved it there, riding motorcycles, running around free. The kids had a blast. Being there was spiritual for me. I felt so much peace in the desert. I love the desert sky. Night time was magical; we cooked and played games. I was not drinking, and was truly enjoying myself for the first time in a long time.

While we were in the desert, the boys and I discussed their dad's drinking and what we could do to help him. We planned to go back home, talk to him, and take him to rehab again. This usually worked, because he had a pattern of drinking until he had no other choice.

My ex-husband and I remained friends after our divorce and did our best to raise our children together. The boys would try to get away with things, playing their father against me, because they did not realize we talked every day. We worked together to make sure we stopped their nonsense right away and laughed about it behind their backs when we caught them. He could be a loving man. I wanted him to be healthy for our boys.

We returned to the Bay Area, and the boys called their dad. He didn't answer. I suggested they go to his house to check on him, but they didn't want to see him drunk. I went to his home, knocked on the door and tried to get in, but he did not answer and the doors were locked. I thought, *Great, he's checked himself into a hospital, rehab, or he is with a friend. He will call us soon.* He always sobered up and called with an apology.

After I hadn't heard from him for a few days, I began to worry more—as I had many times—so I called the police to do a wellness check on him. They often discovered him drunk, perhaps passed out, not answering his phone. They would call to let me know he was okay. He was always mad when I did this, but I cared deeply about him and wanted my boys to have their father.

At ten o'clock I received a call at my office from the police. They asked me to come to his home. I asked, "Why? Is he okay? Is he home?" They would not tell me anything, just insisted I meet them.

I told my brother and he came with me. On the way we talked, hoping my ex-husband was okay, that this time he would quit drinking for good. We arrived at his home and were met by a man coming out of the house. Not knowing who he was, I asked, "Is my ex-husband okay?" When I tried to walk into the house, this man blocked me, saying the police were inside still.

The man I was speaking to was the coroner. He told me my ex-husband had passed away.

Falling into my brother's arms, I lost it. I could not believe my ex-husband was gone. I wanted to see him; I wanted to hug him and tell him it will be okay. You cannot leave me alone with the boys. No!

Maybe this is a mistake, I thought. He will come back if I talk to him and tell him the boys and I need him, that we cannot do this without him.

They would not let me see him. The pain was devastating. I looked at my brother and said, "What about the boys?" As I was crying hysterically, I said, "How do I look in their faces and tell them their dad is gone? How do I do this?" My poor little guys, they were fourteen and sixteen. The pain we inflicted upon them because of alcoholism.

My children's father lost his life at forty-eight-years old due to alcoholism. He died alone in his home, lying on the living room floor for five days. He did not deserve to leave this world by himself. All I could think about was him lying there alone. Was he scared? Had he needed us? Could we have helped him?

He loved his boys with all his heart and my boys loved him. He was a great father: funny and handsome. But he was an alcoholic. He knew his demons and he battled them daily. He talked about dying often. When we were married, he told me he would die young; he told my boys the same.

We always just thought he was just feeling down and never took him serious. He knew his life would end because of drinking, but he would not stop.

He left his boys without a father because he would not look at his addiction honestly. He always thought he could have one more drink. He died with that belief.

I had been sober a little over a month. I had no way of coping with the pain without drinking. My brother drove me back to my office. I jumped into my car and immediately drove to the liquor store. I bought a bottle of chardonnay and drank the whole bottle before telling my sons their father had died. I did not know how else to behave. I am an alcoholic and we drink for the solution. I was ashamed of myself.

I remember the blank stares in their eyes. They did not cry. They stayed numb, just pushing the pain down inside, just like their father and I treated all our pain. They stared at me. I was a mess, but they were scared, in pain, and looking to me for comfort. I tried my best to ease the pain, but I was torn apart. The three of us sat there just saying, "no", shaking our heads, hugging each other, asking, "what do we do now?"

Planning his funeral was the most painful event I have ever had to endure. I included my sons in the planning because I wanted them to have the honor and privilege of planning the perfect funeral for their father. We drove early in the morning to the mortuary to pick out his casket and his urn, for his wish was to be cremated. We chose a gorgeous casket. The urn is a beautifully deigned clock. We picked out a clock because their dad was always yelling at us to be on time. I was always late. My boys thought it would be fitting. I agreed.

While driving, we put on a radio station and it seemed like every song was one he loved. I looked at my oldest son and said, "Wow, your dad must be able to pull some strings in heaven, because this station is playing all his songs." My son looked at me with a smile and said, "I was just thinking, this is dad's music." We had a little laugh. I told my boys, "You know how much your father loves you. He will always be with you." They each said, "I know, mom." Strong little guys. I am blessed.

The service was amazing. My son even said, "Dad went out in style." He did and he deserved it.

The wake was full of all his family and friends, with standing room only. The room was filled with people who loved him and would have done anything for him. As I looked around the room, I thought, *Any of these people here would have helped him if he would have reached out.*

But he did not each out. Like many alcoholics he felt worthless, unloved, and that everyone would be better off without him. He told me many times, "The boys will be better off without me."

Lies are the disease of addiction. Addiction tells you that you are worthless, unloved, a loser, a vagrant, irresponsible, and no one will miss you. That is far from the truth. We all have family, friends, and a fellowship that loves us and will be there for us if we reach out. But we don't. We are stubborn, full of fear, pride and ego.

We are broken, in pain, and lost, but we are good people. In our disease, we push everyone away because of the shame and guilt. We cannot see the truth when we are drinking or using.

Fight for your life and keep fighting for those around you. You are worth it! Your family and loved ones need you.

We miss him every day. My boys would give anything for one more minute with their dad. His sisters, brothers, and cousins miss him and wish they would have done more to help him. Every special occasion is bittersweet.

This is what addiction steals from us if we do not take the disease seriously. When drinking, we are so selfish. We think it is our life and we can live it how we want to, but we do not think about our children, parents, loved ones and friends when we make that statement. We think only of ourselves. I should know, because I said it many times, but I now know better. I see my children's pain and emptiness. Their lives will never be the same without their dad.

We feel the joy of his memory alongside the pain of his absence. He will miss his son's lifetime memories, from getting their driver's licenses to marrying and having children. He'll never see his boys grow up. They will never have their father to ask about life or be able to have him go fishing or golfing with them.

Today I have had the honor of seeing our sons grow into nice young men, something I know their dad would have loved to be a part of. In their short time, together he showed our sons plenty of love and, even though we were divorced, he always told my sons, "You take care of your mother." My boys have taken good care of me, even when I did not deserve their care.

After his death, I wanted to quit drinking. I tried, but could not keep it together. My children were grieving for their father and watching their mother drink away her life. What a sad and disturbing parallel to my own life: the life I lived with my mother's death and my father's drinking. My boys were living the same nightmare I swore I would not put my children through.

Broken in all areas of my life—my marriage, my business, my spirit—I wished I was the one who had died.

The first year after my ex-husband's death was spiritual, magical and heartbreaking. I felt him with me. He seemed at peace, free from the pain of addiction. He could not find his peace here on earth.

He passed away on December fourth. Christmas was coming soon. I wanted the boys to have a good Christmas, to honor their father by living a good life like he would want for them.

One day, close to Christmas time, my son and I stood out in the cold night air, looking at his car. I'd had it fixed up for him and he was thrilled. His car was extra special because his father had picked it out before he died. They'd shopped for months looking for this car.

All I could think about was his dad missing out on Christmas, that now every Christmas would be one without him. I was in so much pain watching my son. He was happy with his car, but lost without his dad. He looked at me with a smile, but the loss was evident behind his beautiful innocent smile.

I wished I could just rewind time. I would have given anything to go back to when we were married. I would have fought harder to give my boys a better life. Maybe, just maybe, he would be alive today and here with us. I had so much guilt inside. My selfish behavior had caused so much pain for the ones I loved.

I felt strange. Suddenly I turned around and saw a shadow on the fence. The shadow moved like my ex-husband, with his distinctive walk, with that slight bend to his back. It was dark and late at night. Where was this light coming from? I looked around to see if a car was coming with the lights on, but nothing was there. He was with us, watching his son. I was frightened and elated at the same time. I did not say a word to my son. He would have thought I was crazy and I did not want to hurt him. But I knew inside his father was with us. I felt his love for our sons. That deep love he had for them could not die.

I turned to go to the shadow, but he was walking away. *Please, please stay with us,* I said to myself. *Please don't leave us. Please.* But he walked the other way and then he was gone.

At night I lay in bed, praying to God to send him back. *God please,* I'd beg, *send him back. It's okay if you made a mistake. I won't tell anyone. Just please give him another chance here on earth.* Today I know that God does not make mistakes.

Many nights I lay in bed thinking about him, embroiled in pain, missing him, feeling the sadness of my children. I was so scared and lonely. How could I go on? Suddenly I felt a kiss on my lips. It was him. I knew the feel of his mustache. A sense of well-being washed over me. He was with us, watching over us.

I hope and pray he is at peace and guiding us in the right direction.

CHAPTER 8

I CAN HANDLE THIS

Life felt stagnant, yet within me resided the feelings that something must change. I wanted a better life.

Of course, I still thought I could overcome alcoholism on my own.

Even though I could not stay sober, my boys were always so loving. They would say, "Keep trying Mom, you will be okay." I wanted to be a good mother, to help my children through their grief, but they were the ones helping me.

I stopped drinking, but never for long. Doctor visits became the norm. When there, I was handed medication for all my symptoms, never discussing the real problem. The doctors just told me take this for depression, that for sleep, the list went on. I never liked pills, but that all changed when I was prescribed Xanax.

I thought, *this is paradise.* I did not have to drink, I just took a little pill and life was good!

Eventually, my brain and my body craved more. I began to mix Xanax with chardonnay, and things progressed fast.

Several times I overdosed and ended up in the hospital and was even taken once by ambulance right in front of my sons. Another time, I fell into a coma for a week. I did not know where to turn and still wasn't able to ask for help; I was spiraling out of control. It wasn't that I wanted to die, but I wanted everything to stop.

In the emergency room one night, the doctor asked me, "What's going on?"

"I can't sleep," I said.

"Not sleeping won't kill you," he said. "But alcohol will. Do you want to die?"

I did not answer him.

Then he said to me the words I will never forget: "How do you know if you die it will be easier?"

I never thought about what happens after we die. I had seen many things in my life that convinced me there is a spiritual life and afterlife. I'd often felt my mother and my ex-husband, and knew they were with me.

What would happen if I took my own life? Raised Catholic, I knew God abhorred suicide. What if things in the afterlife were worse for me? I knew what I faced on earth. I realized I didn't want to die, I didn't want to leave my boys. I just wanted to live in peace.

The doctor referred me to a hospital day treatment program. The next day I started treatment. Librium helped me deal with the week-long withdrawal of detox. I attended some group meetings and lectures, but did not connect with recovery until I walked into a mandatory AA meeting.

I walked into a room full of so many happy people that I thought, *this is the wrong room.* They were laughing and hugging each other. Women came up to me and asked my name, asked if I was new and if I was okay. One of them said, "Hold on honey. You are in for the ride of your life!"

I could not think straight. Detoxing and depressed, thinking I was doomed, I thought, *this is where life brought me!*

They were introducing themselves as grateful alcoholics. My thought was yeah, *you say that because you have nothing else in your life.* I was so wrong and so miserable. I thought happiness was reserved for everyone else but me.

I sat in the meeting because I had to, watching the clock, thinking about my office, all the work I needed to get done.

The speaker was a woman, her story full of pain and struggle. Tears began to flow from my eyes. Her story seemed like my story. I thought, *why didn't my ex-husband connect to AA? He could be here today, sober and happy like many in the room.* The tears felt good. I tried to remember the last time I'd cried, or if I'd ever cried real tears.

That day was a turning point. I no longer felt alone with my pain and suffering. It was such a relief. It felt so good; I felt safe. The feeling of being with others who shared my same problems, but now had happy lives, gave me hope.

After two weeks of treatment, of not drinking, I felt clear and ready to take on my new life.

Saying goodbye to the counselors, telling them, *thank you very much, I feel great,* even writing them a thank you letter, they just looked at me and said, "You know, there is much more to this program."

They tried to stop me, but I told myself I had it all under control. This was just a rough spot for me. I needed to get back to my dysfunctional marriage, company, and life!

Walking out of day treatment with the belief I was cured, I ran right back to my nightmare life with no sponsor, no meetings, and not truly convinced I was an alcoholic. I was drinking within sixty days.

My world became so small. I drank alone in my bedroom, pretending I was not drinking, trying to hide my drinking from my sons, yet they knew. I would buy groceries before going home, take the bottle of wine, put it in my purse, and throw away the receipt. My boys would help me with the groceries bags when I arrived home. I did not want them to see my wine bottle.

I threw the empty bottles in my closet until I had time to bag the bottles and put them in the garbage. To my surprise, I had huge black bags full of empty wine bottles by the end of the week. I'd drag the bag through the house with the clanging noise of the bottles hitting each other, thinking no one knew what I was doing. If this scenario wasn't so devastating to me and my children, it would be comical.

My mind was a mess. They knew everything—everyone in my life knew. Inside the delusion of addiction, I was really living in an exhausting world of my own.

Drinking was draining every part of my life. I could not give a hundred percent of myself to anyone or anything. I was a terrible mother and an irresponsible partner in the company. Every day I just went through the motions, like a robot: go to work, come home, drink a bottle or two of wine, repeat.

One day, I'd had enough. I decided to admit myself to a thirty-day rehab. I chose the rehab my ex-husband went to many times in his life. I missed him so much and wanted to be close to him. In some strange way, this was a way to feel him around me.

Walking into the rehab, still so full of myself, doing this for all the wrong reasons, I looked around, saw shabby décor and the menu featuring pasta and hot dogs. The first thing that came to my mind was, *I don't eat pasta or hot dogs! I am out of here!*

I said to the counselors, "I'm going into town. I'll get a hotel, go to the spa, eat good food, and work out. But I will be back for daily meetings if that will be okay with you?" They looked at me as if I was crazy, and I was. Still trying to run the show and planning my own treatment.

Talk about denial. How delusional. My life was a mess, my children were hurting—and I did not want to eat *pasta?* I didn't eat carbs, but I could drink two bottles of wine a night?

That was my life. Everything was falling apart, and I knew it and felt it, but continually cycled back to this thought: *I'm fine and I can fix this on my own. I'm not a real alcoholic.* I'm better than all those addicts. But the truth was, I was caged in fear. I did not know how to live without alcohol.

How could I possibly think I could take care of myself at this point of my life? My children had just lost their father; my business was failing; and my marriage was a disaster. My drinking damaged everything I loved in my life, yet I thought I could fix my life on my own. That is the power of denial and the disease of addiction. Anything to keep drinking and using.

From a young age, I had taken care of myself. Believing I was strong and independent blinded me from the true power of addiction. I crossed that fine line from user to abuser, from drinker to alcoholic, and I was fighting to regain control. I could not win this fight alone.

I left rehab, waving to the counselors, saying, "See you in the morning!" I rented a hotel room, all ready to detox, relax, eat well, exercise and shine. I was on my way to a better life.

That lasted until lunchtime the next day. I was drinking chardonnay. I met so-called friends and the party was on. My children thought I was getting help in a rehab, but I was out drinking and living it up in Calistoga. Shame flared up. Guilt. Remorse. I drank more and more to quiet the voices in my head.

That innocent glass of chardonnay at lunch led me to waking up in the middle of the night in the emergency room. I had fallen and cracked my head open on the cement in Calistoga. Talk about humiliation and despair.

After being released from the hospital, I went home to face my boys. What a terrible mother. I walked in the door feeling like such a piece of dirt. My boys hugged me and told me they loved me.

With hope, I gave another try at outpatient day treatment. This time, I ended up even more distraught and humiliated. My first time in treatment felt great. This time, even while taking Librium, I didn't feel better. The concussion from my fall was not healing. This turned into vertigo and shooting pains through my head. I thought perhaps I'd had a stroke, and became terrified. I could not read clearly or write my name. Thinking I was permanently damaged was frightening.

Instead of transferring from day treatment to something more intensive, I quit going. Though hard to believe, I was not ready to give up my battle to be normal. The voice inside told me being an alcoholic was shameful and I was defective in some way. I wanted to be normal, work, raise my sons, and drink with my friends. Everyone around me drank, so I should be able to too.

Returning to my business and marriage, convinced I could get better on my own, remaining blind to the alcoholic I was, the farce continued.

CHAPTER 9

LOSING MY HERO

As I tried to put my life together, my father suffered a severe stroke, becoming bedridden and unable to communicate clearly. My father had become my rock; we had developed an unbreakable bond between us. We had been through so much together. We were friends; we worked side by side for almost thirty years; we talked on the phone daily; and went to dinners and took vacations together. He had become everything to me. I'd lost my mother, my sons' father, and was now losing my father. To see him lying in bed, helpless, felt devastating.

One day while visiting my father, I sat next to his bedside, crying, missing his ability to talk with me so much. I needed him. I'd never talked to him about my problems, but I'm sure he knew. He'd watched and tried to help, but he was an alcoholic, so he knew I had to be ready and willing before I could change anything.

During my life, part of my close bond with my father and my

ex-husband came because of the fact we were alcoholics—we knew the suffering caused by the disease of addiction. Only alcoholics and addicts can truly understand what we go through spiritually, mentally, and physically. Too many people are quick to judge alcoholics and addicts. It is special when you find a confidant.

Now, I had lost them both. My father was still alive, but could not talk. As my tears fell, my dad's eyes moved to mine. He gazed at me, then reached over and wiped the tears from my face.

At the time, my father was remarried to a wonderful woman who took good care of him. He was a happy man. I thank God, he was given a second chance at life. He did not waste his sobriety. He created a successful business, remarried, had a little girl, and went to church every day.

He never drank again, and he lived a full life. He often told me, "Honey there is nothing in life that a drink would make better." He was proud of his sobriety and he never looked back on his drinking years.

But now, he was home, lying in bed, day after day. I knew how much pain this brought to his life. We'd had this discussion many times. He'd often said, "I never want to be lying in bed, having someone change my diapers. I want to go quickly." I could not believe his life was ending this way.

He lived two hours away from me. I drove to visit him, and knew in the back of my mind I would drink soon. On the way home, after spending the day with him, the pain was excruciating. Watching him suffer was too much. I pulled over to a restaurant for dinner, and before I could take my coat off and sit down at the table I had ordered a glass of Chardonnay.

Continuing to drink and trying to hold my life together as my father was suffering in and out of the hospital was agonizing. Expecting a call any day that he had passed left me in constant turmoil. I did not know how to hold on or what to hold on to.

My boys had suffered the pain of losing their father, now their grand-father, and now had to watch me drink away the pain. My behavior was selfish—they deserved much better.

There were many special occasions as my father lay suffering in bed. My family would drive to spend the holiday or birthdays with him, but I chose not to go.

I did not want to see him in that state. I thought only of myself and didn't think about the fact that my father looked forward to seeing me. I pushed it all down and forged through my days. Today I would give anything to be by my father's bedside, loving him and thanking him for all he did.

Soon, my father was admitted to the hospital. He had very little time left, as his health was failing quickly. I swore I would be sober when my father crossed over. I quit drinking as his time came near.

One afternoon the hospital called a family meeting. The doctors told us there was nothing more they could do. My father would be discharged the next day and receive hospice care at home. Listening to the doctors discuss the procedure, looking at the huge oxygen tank he would need at home, I had a feeling he would not be going home. I knew he would pass on in the hospital that night.

The last night of my father's life was so emotional. I was sick to my stomach, scared and angry that I had to go through another death.

His room was full of love. His wife, children, grandchildren, and close friends gathered around him. My father looked scared and agitated, I thought. Were there too many people in the room? My father was a very private man. Maybe he wanted to be alone when he crossed over, I thought. The room was bustling with noise, with everyone talking, nurses and doctors coming in and out. No wonder he was agitated. I wanted everyone to leave so I could crawl in bed with him, to be with him as he passed, but they were not leaving.

It was getting late. I wondered if I should drive home or wait until everyone left. I decided to drive home. On the drive home, I continued to feel dizzy and sick to my stomach. I have never felt so strange.

I thought, *should I go back to be with him?* I had such an urge to go back, but I did not listen to myself. I continued to drive home, knowing inside he was leaving me.

Before I left my father that evening, I told my father I loved him very much. I thanked him for being a wonderful father. I am so grateful I was sober and able to say goodbye to the man who loved me and showed so much courage and strength through his lifetime.

I told him, "Don't worry, God will take good care of you."

I kissed him and said goodbye. With tears of love and pain falling down my cheeks, I said to him, "Dad, if you can leave me anything, please leave me your strength."

I needed his strength to get through my life without him.

The next morning, my brother called.

"Are you going to visit Dad today?" he asked.

"Have you called the hospital?" I responded. Deep down, I knew our father had died.

My brother called the hospital, then called me back to say our father had passed away during the night.

He was sober thirty-two years when he passed away.

We prepared for the funeral, and that is when it hit me: I saw my sisters, my father's wife, and many others going through the grieving process without drinking. I thought *I am such a coward to make this about me and drink over it; I should feel this pain.* But of course, I drank.

One night before the funeral I was shopping for a black jacket at Macy's. When I saw a woman in her wheelchair having a hard time getting through an aisle in the store, I went over to help her. As I was pushing her wheelchair, she thanked me and said, "God is going to take good care of you!" Those were the same words I told my father as he lay dying. At first shocked, I brushed it off as a coincidence.

I know now that was not a coincidence. We receive messages every day to help guide us and to help us make the right choices in life, if we are open to receiving them. At that point of my life, I was not open to receiving anything positive.

At my father's funeral, many spoke of what a great man he was and how they respected him. What a contrast to when I was young and all I'd ever heard was, *what a drunk. What a low-life, no-good man.*

Through his many years of sobriety, he had changed his whole life. He had become a good man, a good father, and a good husband. He was forgiven by many. Even my mother's mother forgave him, and they remained close during his life. Perhaps most difficult of all, my father forgave himself.

Many of us have such a hard time forgiving ourselves for the pain and wreckage we cause. We must forgive ourselves so we can be free to live a happy and healthy life and to use our pain and struggles to help others recover.

Witnessing the wonderful things being said about my father at his funeral, I thought, *I want my boys to be proud of me.* I had a vision of one day becoming a good woman.

I had to change. It was time.

This was in October 2010. The country was still in a recession and it was a difficult time.

Drinking every day, I followed my same routine: work, drink, lay in bed. I tried to function, but I just could not move through the pain. It was overwhelming.

Until my father died, I could pretend and move on through life. The pain of my mother's and my ex-husband's death, the abuse, everything I suffered in life, I pushed down in order to move forward. But suddenly I could not do that any longer.

I wanted to mourn and grieve my father. He deserved that. My soul was no longer allowing me to bury my feelings and move on. It felt good to finally want to feel the pain.

Walking into my office was not peaceful any longer. The passion was gone. I resented that fact that I had to be there instead of mourning my father. I knew it was time to leave the company.

It was now December. Two months had passed since my father died, though it felt like an eternity.

Every day I said, *I cannot do this any longer.*

I thought about ending my life, but I'd made a promise to my boys' father that I would take care of the boys. Before his funeral, I'd written a letter to him and stuck it in his suit pocket. I had to honor that promise.

CHAPTER 10

WHY NOT ME?

A ttempting to put another dreadful year behind me, I planned a trip to Lake Tahoe to ring in 2011 and celebrate a new year with my boys. Drinking and depressed, I thought about another year of living in this state, feeling if something did not change I would not make it through the year.

We arrived in Lake Tahoe, at a wonderfully picturesque area and a comfortable cabin. The boys were excited to snowboard. We went out and all had a great time. The second day of the trip, I did not want to go with the boys to snowboard, explaining to them that I could use a day to relax in the cabin, read, and stay warm. They hesitantly agreed. They knew me, but probably figured I couldn't get into a whole lot of trouble in the middle of the woods without any alcohol. So off they went in the truck with my husband and his children.

At last, I had a whole day to myself to relax and unwind. That did not last long because I got bored quickly. Then I remembered seeing a diner down the road as we drove in. I felt hungry, so I got dressed in my snow gear and off I went, walking a mile down the road in freezing snow. We alcoholics persevere. When we want a drink, we find a way.

The diner had a nice warm bar, dark and rustic, with the smell of old alcohol. I loved those types of bars. I ordered my glass of wine, and thought, *This is going to be a great day.* As I sat there and drank, speaking to others at the bar, I talked about how much I loved my children and how thankful I was for their love.

One of the women said, not too eloquently, "If you love them so much, why aren't you with them today?" At first, I was furious. Who was this woman to say such a thing? Then reality hit. She was right. What was I doing? I should be with them, not at a bar.

I'd always talk about loving my boys and being a business owner and a great woman. I was full of it! My life was one big lie. *I am done with the pretense,* I told myself. *I am an alcoholic, a terrible mother, and a bad business partner.* Somehow that felt good to say, but this time I mean it.

I wanted sobriety, but like many things in my life, I thought it was a great thing, but one I could never attain. I told myself I could not be happy, healthy and sober. That was for other people, I was not that kind of person.

Then I began to think, *Why not me?* I see people who are happy and healthy, living full, fun lives, people who at times in their life struggled with addiction.

Why not me? Why can't I get better?

The answer came as I sat in that dive bar in Lake Tahoe. I was not doing any work. I was not addressing my addiction. I was not going to counseling, meetings, or reaching out for help.

The people who had peace and contentment worked hard for it. I was just lying around feeling sorry for myself, thinking this was what life had in store for me. Playing the victim, not accepting I had the power to change my life.

I got ready for my long walk back to the cabin with a sense of hope. I would change my entire life. Suddenly my boys, step-children and husband walked into the diner. My youngest son said to me, "The search party is here, Mom. Let's go back to the cabin." They had come back to the cabin early and found it empty. They did not have to look far to find me. They were upset, but we did manage to find a little humor in my escapade. They were shocked I'd walked that far in the snow, and shook their heads at me.

When we were settled in that night in the cabin, I said to my boys, "You know what? This year is going to be the year of *why not me?* This year is going to be different."

They looked at me and said, "Oh, Mom, go to sleep." They had heard that proclamation before. Many times before. I promised my children so much and never came through with any of the promises. Especially after today, they were not having it! But deep down, I could feel a shift. It would be different this time, I just knew.

The weekend was over and a new year began. I walked back into my business and my dysfunctional marriage, but I knew things were going to change. How would I begin?

Night after night, I built up the courage to change. Then, as many say, something just came over me and that was it—life as I knew it was over. It was time to change.

In February of 2011, I resigned. After thirty-two years of working in the family business and having a great life financially, I'd had enough. The fighting, the disrespect between my brothers and me—I just knew I could not stay. I knew, too, they needed someone they could count on, and that was not me. I was irresponsible and not productive. Being on my own for the first time in thirty-two years was terrifying, but I had a feeling deep down inside this was the right thing to do.

At forty-eight, my whole life vanished, everything that made me complete was gone. Forty-eight was a scary age because my mother died at forty-eight, my sons' father died at forty-eight and now I was facing my mortality at forty-eight. Could I change? If so, how?

The business had been my identity throughout my life. Now I was unemployed.

Fooling myself for so long with material success, I'd thought I was living life as it was intended: work hard, make money, raise your children. Along the way I neglected my needs and my happiness.

Losing everything, I was forced to finally take an honest look at myself, and where my addiction had taken me. I was stripped down. I had a choice: to accept this life, continue as I had been on this destructive path, or rise up and fight to rebuild my life.

What to do now? I had no job and no money coming in. I thought, *I'm going to move to Los Angeles.* Why? Who knows? I was looking for an escape. That wouldn't help, I realized. Anywhere I went, I would take me with me. I did not want to be the old me, the addicted me, any longer.

I sat in my room alone, asking myself what I should do. The next thing I did was pick up the phone and call the treatment center, the same place I'd been to two times before but never finished. I thought they would say, "Sure, Karen, here is a referral for another place. Good luck to you."

Instead, the counselor on the other end of the phone said," When can you be here?"

"In the morning," I said.

There was a half-bottle of chardonnay in my room, so like any good alcoholic, I had to finish it. As I drank the last glass of my favorite wine, I looked at the woman in the mirror and hated what I saw. I hated what alcohol had done to my life, my children's life, my ex-husband and my father.

That night, I fell asleep with a sense of relief. The next day, I walked into the treatment center, and the counselors had it out with me, "One more relapse and you are in for thirty-day residential," they said.

I agreed and signed the paperwork. Now I had permission to work on me. No distractions, no business to run back to, no marriage to save. I was finally free to heal. I made the decision to fight for my life, for me, and for who I wanted to be for my sons. What a beautiful battle it has been.

CHAPTER 11

DROPPING THE FAÇADE

The years to follow that miracle day of March 22, 2011 have been filled with, pain, sorrow, happiness, guilt, remorse and a new sense of spirituality. I have learned to love, live and feel freedom. But it has not been easy, not at all.

Arriving each day to treatment excited and willing, happy and upbeat, many would say *what pink cloud are you on? Do not get too attached to the feeling, life shows up.* I did not listen, I was sincerely happy, for the first time in my entire life.

I was introduced to a wonderful woman who became my sponsor. I put her through the fire the first year, still thinking I knew everything and that I was not a true alcoholic and not as bad as many of the people in treatment. I could make myself up to look the part of a woman in control on the outside, but I could not fix the inside.

In early recovery, still pretending, I arrived at treatment each day dressed up like I was going to the office: high heels, a skirt, hair done, the whole uniform.

And of course, I was in love with a counselor. In my fantasy head, he loved me too and knew I was different; we were going to get married and live a happy life together, as soon as I was finished with treatment. I was a mess still, with no idea how to give up the façade. That did not last long.

Life got tough.

Many days, I did not want to go to meetings, and all I could think about was drinking, but I had commitments: I was the coffee maker, greeter, and secretary. I'd tell myself, *after this stupid meeting I am going to drink.*

As usual, in the meeting I would hear something that gave me hope, and would witness others going through painful situations sober. Some had lost their spouse, or a friend, others had lost their children, yet they were there in a meeting sober, working through the pain with others who truly cared about them. This put my small problems in perspective.

Days that were extremely hard, I went to meetings, even though I was struggling emotionally and feeling like I couldn't go on any longer. In those moments, I felt a warmth come over me, almost like a hug from someone you loved, letting me know *just hold on, good things are coming.*

I had a little spark of hope inside, wanting to be healthy, happy and sober. I kept moving forward, not wanting to go back to the woman I had been in the past.

I began to work on myself, looking inside. It was frightening to be so raw and honest. To feel such pain, to acknowledge the pain I had caused others. Suddenly realizing I was not this perfect little victim, I had a part in my demise.

The first year was a rough road, and I found myself constantly saying *I want my life back!* Naturally, I attacked things stubbornly, trying to put it all together quickly, forcing my way, not letting things unfold organically. The struggle to let go of my ego, pride and selfishness was tough. I'd hoped all I had to do was quit drinking and life would be perfect. I had no idea that I drank because I could not live life in all its imperfection.

Even though down deep I knew my marriage was over, I believed I should still try to be a good wife and save my marriage. Recognizing my part in our problems, I thought, if I changed he would change too.

However, being sober and learning to live an honest life, I saw immediately that he wanted no part in honesty, hard work, or helping me financially. Now that I was sober, the money train was over for him.

He found a new young woman and left the country to be with her, leaving me in financial ruin, in care of my two sons and his son. The house went in and out of foreclosure. Bills piled up from his construction business that I'd helped him start by signing for equipment, trucks, and tools.

But I was not innocent. When drinking, I loved to be the big shot. *Sure, you can use my excellent credit for your business.* This gave me a feeling of self-worth. I also knew if I did not sign the paperwork he would harass me. I gave in, knowing inside I wasn't making the right decision. He knew how to manipulate me: he'd take me to a fancy restaurant with plenty of wine before asking me to sign for his equipment. I'm sure I bought dinner too!

Drinking, I did not listen to my instincts. My body was always sending me messages and guidance. I chose to drown the messages out with alcohol. It seemed like a much easier way to live at the time. Learning to live with integrity is difficult and uncomfortable, but the results are incredible. I was beginning to believe in myself . . . a true miracle.

The pain of facing all of this alone was extreme, and I wanted to drink for the relief, but I thought about where drinking would take me. I did not want to live that life again.

It was not easy. I thought about how he'd just left me and the kids, and how he was on a white-sand beach, falling in love with another woman, happy and loving life. While I struggled.

But a little voice kept speaking to me: *Keep going forward. You know what he is doing to her—the same thing he did to you. He is using her for everything he can and then he will move on.*

Not knowing how to get through the pain, I tried everything, meetings, talking to others, walking. These seem to help, but it was still killing me inside.

I thought, *this is sobriety. I am doing all the right things and look at my life, —financially ruined and alone on a Saturday night in my room.*

I took out my yoga mat and turned on a DVD. Others told me how yoga helped them get through pain. Just as I was trying to do a yoga pose, my son walked in my room.

"Oh, no, are you really doing YOGA!"

I looked at him and started to cry. "Yes, I am doing yoga, feeling like the biggest loser." Then we both looked at each other and started laughing. At that moment, we both knew everything was going to be all right. As he left the room, he said, "You got this Mom!"

The boys knew my pain and they were in pain also. My husband was their step-father, a huge part of their life for over fifteen years. They felt the pain of the abandonment too, but they told me, "Mom, we will be better off without him." They were furious at him for leaving us during such hard times.

Today I receive phone calls and texts from him. He tells me he loves me and misses me. He tells me the affair is over between him and the other woman. Yet the next day on social media

I see pictures of the two of them together. He is still lying and cheating. I am so blessed to be away from him, out of the abuse and addiction.

His girlfriend sends me messages, asking what we are talking about. I feel for her. I know exactly how she feels. In the beginning of their relationship I tried to warn her, but she did not want to hear anything from me, just as I was warned by others in the beginning of our relationship and chose not to listen.

She is just like me, thinking she is different and he will change for her. I know this is a common mistake that men and women make when entering a new relationship. We ignore the red flags and pay a huge price for that in many ways.

I should have left at the first hit, the first lie, or the first affair, but I was sick and stuck in my own nightmare. I forgive myself and do not beat myself up about it. He is on his own path and I wish him happiness and peace. He will never be in my life again.

I also had to deal with the agony of being raped when I was fourteen. How do I get through the pain and humiliation sober? This man abused me, an innocent little fourteen-year-old girl. He walked away free, to hurt more innocent girls. I felt the guilt of not speaking up and not valuing myself. But, I was fourteen, I was frightened, and dealing with the chaos of my family life.

I had to forgive, but I will never forget. Dealing with the pain and humiliation was paralyzing. I know he set my life on a path of destruction when he raped me. I had to put myself first and learn to love me with all the wounds, scars and brokenness.

I do not need to retaliate or hold on to pain any longer, he took away my innocence, but I am free to help others who have gone through the same pain. I will never let him win. He is a criminal and rape is about power. I took my power back, today I am happy, free and beautiful just the way I am.

I had to be free, and the only way I now know to be free is to feel the feelings and go through the process. All my life I pushed pain down and numbed my feelings. I ran and I drank. Today, I never want to jeopardize my sobriety. I know I must feel my true feelings, both good and bad. If I do not deal with my feelings, they will manifest somewhere else. Life has a way of dealing with you. I found that out over and over.

All my life I did not look at sex as an enjoyable act, and I longed to learn how to look at intimate relationships in a healthy way. I had to take my body and my mind back. This was hard, but today I am worthy and loveable.

In the past I did not know why I let men treat me terribly, to this day I must be careful to excuse bad behavior from them. I am an honest and loving woman and some men easily take advantage of my kindness. Every day I remind myself I am worth being loved and that I must take care of myself!

It took a lot of time and work on myself to get to this place of peace and forgiveness. Sometimes the sober but still sick part of me missed the chaos I had with my husband. I missed the overblown, romantic part of him, but I knew it was all phony, with nothing sincere, true or healthy. Not able to live in dishonesty any longer, my spirit was healing and I craved peace, honesty, and sincere love.

On my journey of healing, I had to take an honest look at my life. The choices I made, the pain I caused and the lies I told others—but especially the lies I told myself. Honesty was difficult. It hurt. It was humiliating and so humbling. Alcohol had lied to me. And now that I could no longer believe its lies, I recognized I was sick, hurt, and so full of fear.

Setting out on my path to freedom, I filed for divorce—scary but exhilarating at the same time. Getting honest was painful, but it felt good. For years, I had made excuses for my marriage. For years, I thought

I deserved to be abused.

I did not deserve to be abused. No woman does.

But I did see my part in the madness and that is when I learned to forgive.

Eventually, I apologized to him. I had hurt him with my words and actions, and I had to see that and feel his pain. That does not excuse what he did to me, but I had to take responsibility for *my* actions. This set me free.

He has not acknowledged or apologized, to this day. He will not admit or take responsibility for abusing me. I accept that I will probably never receive an apology from him.

Little by little I was healing, learning to be honest and learning to live without drinking or using any substance to numb my feelings. When uncomfortable feelings swept over me, the pain was excruciating. I had to grieve properly for my father, my mother, and my ex-husband. When they passed away, I numbed myself with alcohol. The feelings had just been repressed; they had not disappeared. Now they were surging forward.

I missed them all so much, wishing they could be a part of my new venture in life, the new woman I was becoming. Sober, I cycled through the sadness, anger and heartbreak.

Then peace came to me. After truly feeling the feelings, I could see that I loved them and they loved me. We all did the best we could do living in the chaos of addiction. Instead of the pain and the loss of their lives, I chose to live with their love. I choose to honor their lives by living a healthy and happy life.

To honor my mother, I will be a good mother.

To honor my father, I will show my boys the strength and courage my father displayed with his thirty-two years of sobriety.

To honor my sons' father, I will help alcoholics and addicts in his name.

By honoring their lives, my life has purpose, a life permeated with love and caring. Each day I am privileged to open my eyes and say, "What can I do today to be a blessing in the lives of others?"

I prayed that my parents were together in heaven. I thought about it often: Would my mother forgive my father if they met in the heaven?

One night I woke up to see my parents together looking young and in love. My mother wore her wedding dress. My father's face shone handsome and young. I wiped my eyes and took another look. They stood there in my room looking at me, smiling. I will always think of my parents finally in love, happy and healthy together.

I look back on my childhood and know that my father loved me very much. He was an alcoholic and learned from his father how to survive in this world, just as I learned from him. I hated the dysfunction, yet I put my children through the same dysfunction.

Today I am trying to break the cycle of addiction in my family by showing my sons that life does not have to be chaos and dysfunction. I am here for them and present. We talk, we laugh and we grow together Through good times and bad times, we are here for each other. I show them by my actions each day that life is good.

CHAPTER 12

ON MY OWN

On my own, and determined to make it financially, I began a career in real estate. I was still living the life of chasing success and money. That is all I'd known, but now my heart was not in sync with that lifestyle. Deep down, I wanted to help others, to pass on this gift of sobriety I had been given.

I could not get rid of the feeling that I had a purpose now. Because of addiction, people were hurting and families being torn apart. What if I could help? What if I could help families heal, help women be powerful, and children be safe? That was my dream.

Only three months sober, I told others my dream was to open a sober-living home and help others recover. People would say, "How about you get sober first?" I thought I was cured. Little did I know I had a lot of growing up to do . . . and still do!

I had wonderful times in my life, traveling to many exotic places, enjoying friends, family and experiences. But drinking robbed me of the true feeling of the places I visited, the people around me, and my family. I was pre-occupied with getting to the right feeling, trying to reach that special point where I felt good. But I would always overshoot the mark, drink too much, and miss the true experience. Now I needed to learn how to enjoy traveling and socializing without drinking.

One afternoon I took a drive to the coast, stopping at the beach. The beach was crowded with people, enjoying themselves. I thought, *why are people at the beach on a Tuesday? Why are they off work?* That amazed me and showed how small my life had become while drinking. I thought everyone was in an office all day. I was beginning to see just how huge our world is, and what others do to enjoy their lives. This realization was exciting and I wanted more now that I was free to make my own decisions, without any business demands, without a husband, and most importantly, without addiction controlling my life.

But with life there are always challenges. Two years into sobriety, I did not like where my life was going. I was not living my purpose, but I didn't know how to let go of the old me and trust in the new me.

Living with my sons and stepson, three boys ages eighteen through twenty-two, I had expenses to cover. Food, insurance, home and schooling were expensive. My real estate career was not taking off.

I was in trouble financially.

I sought a break from the stress. I didn't want to drink, but I felt a void in my life, so I took a few days off and went alone to Santa Catalina Island. I love the ocean. It clears my mind and gives me peace.

Alone in my hotel room, I thought, *I can have a few drinks. No one will know. I will just quit when I go home again.* It was late and I was too tired to go out, so I thought, *I will drink tomorrow.*

I fell asleep with the TV on. In the middle of the night, I woke to Pastor Joel Osteen's show.

"God gave you a gift," he was saying. "It's okay if you don't want it. He will take it back. But there is no promise he will give it back to you again. There are others who will appreciate his gift."

It felt like he was talking directly to me. In the space of a minute, those words changed my life.

I told myself, *My life is a gift. My sobriety is a gift. I am not giving them back.*

The next morning, I woke with a new desire to live my life each day in faith. Good days and bad days, I decided I would choose to have faith that things would work out just as they were meant to be.

Instead of spending the day in a bar drinking and ruining my life once again, I went kayaking on the ocean, where the sparkling water and sea air caressed my soul.

Today, I listen to Pastor Joel Osteen. I learn and grow with faith and encouragement from his sermons.

CHAPTER 13

BUILDING MY DREAM

Finally, I opened my first sober-living home, "The Summer's House", after my ex-husband, as his last name was Summers. I wanted his life to live on and our boys to have something of their father.

The home was beautiful and had such a peaceful feeling to it. As the house started to fill, I was in heaven. This was my dream come true: helping recovering alcoholics and addicts. I had so many plans. We would all be happy, healthy, eating nutritious food, exercising, loving God and living sober—just like me!

Wow, was I in for a surprise. You cannot change anyone. They must need to change, want to change, and be willing to do the work. This was not the case with many people who came to the house. Many wanted nothing to do with recovery. It was painful to see the disrespect some had for God, AA, and, at times, for me.

Eventually, though, magic began to happen, as exhausting as the experience was. I wanted to heal everyone with love and compassion, and some people started to respond. I witnessed people in the house coming to the rescue of others. I loved to see that. To me, it was growth to see others care and show their feelings.

The events that took place in the house were heartbreaking, hysterical, and frustrating. We all grew from the good times, and the bad times in the home. People came and went; I was introduced to others who were in need, but not all wanted the help. That didn't matter. I was prepared to offer comfort if they chose to accept it.

There was drama in the house, too. My boys would always tell me, *"You must make a movie about this stuff!"* At times, we in the house had a lot of laughs over situations that took place. After the dust settled, we would talk about what happened. Sometimes it was funny, but we knew inside this was alcoholism rearing its head.

Many of us get sober, regain the trust of our family and friends, get jobs back and think, *I am doing well. I am going to have a drink to celebrate* . . . and destroy all the progress made. This is the vicious cycle of addiction. Until we admit to ourselves that we are alcoholics and addicts and that we can never drink or use again, we continue the wreckage in our lives and hurt those around us.

At times, the behavior of those in the house baffled me. I couldn't understand why they did not want to change. But of course, it had taken me years to come to this understanding, and each person has their own journey.

Today I spend time with a few of the people who were in the house. They are the lucky ones, for they remained sober. Their lives are happy and healthy. One man, who had been a huge challenge, let go of blaming and complaining and is now getting married, exceling at work, and has a renewed and wonderful relationship with his family.

He is a different person, and realizes his faults. That is difficult for many to do, but what a difference it makes in a person's life when they take one-hundred percent responsibility for the good, and the bad that happens and learn from it. Miracles do happen!

Many treatment programs teach us about the disease of addiction, but do not get to the root of the pain in twenty-eight days. I want to bring back people's passion for life. We are all born with something to do here on earth. The best gift in life is to find your passion and live it.

The people who came through the house were wonderful, intelligent, and loving human beings. They had families that loved them and tried so hard to help, but they pushed it all away.

One man was a finance wizard. He had a supportive ex-wife and two beautiful young daughters. When his ex-wife brought the children to the house for a visit, his daughters were so happy to see their father sober and doing well. His ex-wife was hoping this was the time he would stay sober.

I wanted Bill to stay so we could help him. I'd take him to meetings, pick him up from work, and try to keep him interested in sobriety. He seemed to be doing well. One day as I was eating dinner downtown through the restaurant window I watched him walk by, clearly drunk. I was used to this, having been through it myself. I understood. Most of the people in the house would relapse and then come back to try again.

Not Bill. He called me from a hotel in Las Vegas and said, "I am going to drink myself to death." I reminded him what he had in his life to be thankful for: his daughters, solid employment, his friends. But he could not see the beauty that was right in front of him—he was neck-deep in his addiction.

Not long afterwards, I received word that Bill did, indeed, drink himself to death in a sleazy motel outside the strip in Las Vegas.

In another heartbreaking instance, a father brought his son to the home. His son was twenty-two years old and was addicted to opioids.

I sat with the father as his son settled in his room. We talked about the pain of addiction and what loved ones go through. He was torn. He knew he needed to break all ties with his son for his well-being and his son's recovery, but love is a powerful emotion. He loved his son, yet he was exhausted from the pain and abuse his son had put him and his family through.

When we love someone with an addiction, we want to help. We do not want to see our loved ones go through pain and struggle. We offer money, food and shelter. We put our health and well-being aside, it is exhausting, not only for the addict but the ones who love them. As hard as it is to walk away, it is sometimes the only way an addict can finally reach the bottom he or she needs to reach to finally say, "I am done!" To then begin to do the work required to live a sober and happy life.

We all must walk through the pain and suffering until we are completely done and willing to change. Many addicts never change. They end up in prison or they lose their life to the disease of addiction. We can change, but we must make the decision for ourselves.

His son did not stay in the home. Instead, he left to run the streets. I spoke with his father a month after his son left my house. He told me what happened a week after we met.

One night, as he was walking to his car in a dark shopping center parking lot, he was grabbed from behind, held tightly with a gun stuck in his back. He was terrified, thinking he was going to lose his life.

As soon as the thief said, "Give me all your money, or I will kill you," his heart sank. He recognized the voice immediately. It was his son. His son was robbing him at gunpoint. His son was so high on drugs, he did not know he was robbing his own father.

He said, "Michael, it's me, your dad. Please do not hurt me." Michael ran off, without a word. Unfortunately, this was not enough to change Michael, but it was enough for his father to finally change the locks and buy an alarm system. He had to make the decision to keep his son away from him and the rest of the family. He prays each night that one day soon his son will reach out for help. He wants to see his son sober, living a healthy and happy life.

I witnessed extreme heartbreak from parents, spouses and siblings trying to save their loved ones. Addiction tears through families and leaves open wounds.

Addiction is not the moral weakness and lack of willpower that society thinks it is. That stigma must be broken. It is a powerful disease. If it was easy to quit the addiction more people would, but it is not easy. Addiction is a disease; people die every day from substance abuse.

Yes, over the years the attitude toward addiction has improved, but we need much more attention to mental illness, emotions, and past experiences and their relationship to addiction. Far too many beautiful souls are lost to this disease because of pride, fear and isolation.

Many people die because they are afraid to reach out, because they fear being judged for having a disease.

As a society, we must help ease the feelings of judgement by understanding and comforting an individual with addiction instead of judging them.

CHAPTER 14

FINDING MY STRENGTH

The sober living home had been running for three years. People would come in the house and comment on how peaceful it was. Believe me, at times it was anything but peaceful! Still, I loved every minute of it.

The financial mistakes from my past and my ex-husband leaving me with his business debts started to bury me. The creditors were ruthless. I worked relentlessly to try to receive help from the banks, but they wanted the house to settle the debts.

This was in the height of the recession, when banks were taking homes that owners worked all their lives to be able to buy. Families were being kicked out of their homes with no regard or help.

Many families became homeless, or were living in their cars with their children. I watched this on the news and it made me furious. How can we as a country let this happen to others?

The homes that were taken over from the bank sometimes sat vacant for months, sometimes years. Why? Many homeowners tried to work with the banks, but the banks would not see the human side of the pain they were causing. I fought for my home with the thought of all the innocent people who lost their homes. I walked into the courtroom and lawyer's office with that conviction.

I wanted my boys to keep the home their father owned at the time he passed away. I hired a lawyer, who was also a friend, to handle his affairs. He was having personal problems and did not file the documents on time after taking my case, so I lost to the banks. I was upset and I tried to fight with another attorney but it was too late.

The banks took over, and before I could clean it out, the service team hired by the bank cleared out all my ex-husband's belongings, along with trash and anything else they found, and threw it all into his nice SUV truck that was parked in his garage. This was unacceptable behavior. I couldn't understand how they could be so unfeeling. They knew he had just passed away and that he had children that lived in the home with him. Now I had my own battle to fight.

I had to claim bankruptcy to keep the creditors away. It was humiliating. My whole life I'd prided myself on being responsible and having excellent credit. Now in sobriety, I was dealing with the past. *I was dealing with it.* I was not numbing out or pushing it away. I was there, standing in my life, feeling the heartbreak, but facing reality.

As I was going through Chapter 13 bankruptcy, it was discovered my debts were too high. I needed to go through a Chapter 11, which is a higher level, reconstructive type of bankruptcy. The problem now was the attorneys wanted twenty-thousand dollars just to take my case. I did not want to pay the attorney fees; I wanted to use the funds to save my home.

Many told me to just give up, to lose the house and start over. I said,

"No way." One thing my father taught me in business is to keep going even if they say no. Keep fighting if you know you're right. I watched the house as the value increased. I knew if I could hold on, I could sell for a profit.

I became my own attorney and filed Chapter 11 on my own. I studied the laws, spending hours at the law library, and learned how to type up the pleadings, then drove to San Francisco and filed documents on time with the courts. The judge, the trustee, and many others watched me and told me repeatedly, "You need a lawyer." I agreed, but proceeded to handle my case. I had faith that what I was doing was right.

As I have stated, alcoholics are strong, intelligent, and persistent. We must be to stay alive in our disease. Now I was using that same courage, but applying it in a positive manner to help me fight.

In court, I fought against the bank and other creditors, staying honest and accurate with the facts. I won the judgements. As I walked out of the courtroom, others waiting their turn said, "Right on, you did it!" One man said, "I am fighting for my home and you gave me hope." That made me feel good. We need to help each other and show strength to those who need it.

After the court hearings, I walked out onto the street in San Francisco, shaking my head in disbelief. I could not believe the mess I was in. As I walked away from winning the last round with the banks, I found a shiny penny in the street.

I believe when I find a penny it is from my angels in heaven, letting me know everything is going to be all right. To this day, when I find pennies, I look up in the sky and say thank you. I know everything is going to be okay.

The judge was stern but fair. Many people told me to be careful with her. I liked her and I believe she trusted me. She gave me a huge chance to make it. In the end, she had a smile on her face as I walked out of her courtroom for the last time. I am forever grateful for her, she gave me a break when things for me were at their worst. After the long process, I was not able to keep my home, but I was able to sell it at a profit and walk away with a little bit of dignity.

In AA, I learned to be honest, to trust God and to take action. I will use the profits from the house to open another sober living treatment center. That is my dream, to offer help to those in need.

CHAPTER 15

LESSONS LEARNED

Looking back on my life, I have endured a lot, but through the struggles and losses, hope and perseverance have made me into the woman I am today. Waking up without a hangover and searching for a bottle or a pill is a distant memory. I wake up where I am supposed to be and with whom I'm supposed to be with. Even if I wake up alone, it's okay. Today I do not need to have a man to complete my life. I am happy.

I turned my struggles into successes, for internal peace and happiness is my perception of success. Happiness is a decision. I choose each day to live in a state of gratitude. It takes a lot of patience with myself and others, but the rewards are astonishing.

I no longer resist change, instead I look at growth and change in a positive manner. Fear held me back from living a fulfilling life. I have the courage to tell my true story, to take full responsibility for where my life is at every moment. I make changes to improve my life if I am not feeling satisfied. I no longer accept or make excuses for my unhappiness.

Today my sons and I go out to meals. We take vacations together, just the three of us. We laugh, we tell each other our problems, our dreams. We support each other. We often say, "Man, have we gone through it!"

Yes, we have gone through it, and those two guys have stayed right by my side.

I love them with all my heart and today I can show them real love in return. I hope we will break the cycle of addiction in our family.

Pain and struggling have taught us so much; they have shown us we are strong and we can get through anything together. I am blessed that my sons forgave me and want to be in my life. I put them through a lot of pain, but I always told them how much I loved them and how much I wanted to be a good mother. I did not know how to be one, until now.

Today, I feel the ease of life, walking around feeling so carefree. Sometimes I think, *Did I forget something?* Then I remember: I'm not carrying around the addiction, the pain, the guilt and the feeling of unworthiness. That's a weight I carried on my shoulders for many years.

I am proud of my faith in God. Many people say, "You alcoholics cause so much damage in the lives of those you love—and then you find Jesus and we are all supposed to forgive and forget."

I understand their feelings, but if they lived an addicted life, they would not judge. Only alcoholics and addicts know the pain and suffering we withstand. The agony of not knowing how to stop drinking. Of feeling totally alone.

People often say, "Just stop drinking. Grow up and get responsible." We wish we could. We aren't having fun drinking. We are dying inside and cannot stop until we have a miracle in our life, a moment when we finally say, *I am done* for the last time. Then we work each day to live a happy sober life.

Most people live their life with a belief in God or a higher power. Those who don't believe in something: themselves, their family, their purpose. They have something that keeps them living a healthy, fulfilling life.

Many alcoholics and addicts have no such belief, no such trust in life. Instead they have a black hole that cannot be filled. We search outside ourselves to find peace: we drink, do drugs, over eat anything to help break the pain of addiction. Until we find sobriety, we are lost.

I never felt comfortable in life. I could be in the most beautiful places with people I loved and still have the feeling of unease and lack . . . until I found my spiritual side. Today I can be in the best place or the worse place, but inside me I am at peace and my heart is full.

I know I am not doing this on my own. I am blessed, and will treasure my gift every day of my life. Six years ago, I wanted to die. Today I pray I have enough time on earth to do the things I want to do in my life. When I do pass away, I will be at peace because I've lived my life, my purpose, and left it all on the field.

When I started my recovery, I was forty-five pounds overweight. When the fogged clear and I looked at myself, I thought, *Who is that woman in my mirror?* Drinking, I was blind to what I was doing to myself. I had always been in great shape, but drinking and eating away my feelings left me overweight and with health problems.

I started right where I was, accepting I was overweight. Beginning with small changes in my diet, adding daily exercise, and drinking water. Taking my time and realizing I had a long way to go made the process of watching my body change a pleasant experience. Before, I would hate how I looked and just bury the feeling and buy bigger pants! I happily donated my clothes to a local charity after six months.

In the beginning, I walked a lot. That helped not only with my health but with the high anxiety I felt when I first stopped drinking.

I joined Zumba classes when I was a little stronger and then I joined a gym. Slowly I restored my body and my energy, and began to feel better and look better—and loved the feeling.

Getting back in shape was tough, but it made me feel so much better. Losing five pounds was great. Then another five pounds and another. In one year, I lost those forty-five pounds. Today, six-and-a-half years later, I have kept the weight off and feel fantastic.

My doctors are amazed. When drinking, my blood tests results were not good: high sugar, cholesterol, and overweight. I was offered pills for everything, even my mood. Today I have blood work done and my doctors say, "You are like a twenty-year-old."

Sobriety, exercise, food, and sunshine is the best medicine I know.

I want to be able to enjoy life, but today I have control and I do not crave the bad stuff. Once you start to live your life feeling good, you do not want to change that path.

I have found a passion for hiking and being outdoors. I am alive in nature. I hike mountains that are as high as 10,000 feet, and take in some of the most beautiful views. When I was drinking it was an ordeal to get out of bed to take a shower.

We are all broken somewhere. But we can change and change is within us. We can reach our goals, with patience, strength and a good sense of humor. To laugh at myself is one of my favorite joys in life.

CHAPTER 16

LOOK OUT FOR ONE ANOTHER

know that it is easy to say, *Just be happy and peaceful as we go through life.* When I say this, I mean it, but when life gets tough, it's necessary to dig deep into my strength. I am so grateful I have learned how to live through the darkest times without drinking or taking a drug to numb my feelings.

Recently I witnessed the pain and struggle of a good friend. We were living together at the time. His brother was having a hard time in his marriage and came to stay with us. The first time I met him, I thought, *What a fun and nice guy.* Good looking, intelligent, and a successful business owner.

He had a wife, two children, brothers, sisters and a mother who all loved him very much. He owned and operated a successful business. Everything that society states we should have to be happy in life. To look at him you would envy his life.

The day after I met him, he went to his mother's house and shot and killed himself. To witness the pain and suffering his family endured after his death has been heartbreaking.

To hear his brother crying in the night from the pain of missing his brother, to see his children distraught, and his poor mother in such agonizing pain is, in one word, devastating. Yet this happens to families every day. He walked around with a secret, with pain and suffering that many cannot imagine. He did not seek help because he was proud and felt he should be able to fix his problems on his own. I know that feeling.

This man could be alive today, enjoying his family and friends and the life he fought so hard to build for himself and his family to enjoy—if he sought help and was immediately helped. The day before he killed himself he had called his psychiatrist and was told he could be seen the next day. This was not good enough. How we view and treat mental illness needs improvement.

Mental illness is such a huge problem in our society, but it carries the stigma of shame. Alcoholism is, in my opinion, a form of mental illness. Those of us who struggle with alcoholism have always heard the whispers behind our backs; we know how we are viewed. Because of this stigma many people don't seek help. They try and live their lives without medication or therapy because society says people with mental illnesses are weak, lazy and crazy.

Until his death, I assumed suicide was reserved for alcoholics and addicts. Our culture presses this assumption. While many people try to cope with mental illness through alcohol and drugs, some have never touched these substances. No matter the source, many people in deep distress do not tell anyone because they do not want to be viewed as weak, damaged or crazy. That was true for me, too.

We all need to examine our beliefs and try to purge ourselves of ignorance or insensitivities. Mental illness is just like any other illness. It can be diagnosed and treated, and we can get better.

The most important thing we can do to help those who suffer from mental illness or addiction is to get them help as soon as possible while showing them love and understanding. Just take the time to listen. This can save a life.

If you are suffering and contemplating suicide, reach out. There is help. You can be treated. You can live a happy and healthy life. Your family and friends do not deserve to live a life in pain. Suicide—whether it involves actively killing yourself or passively drinking yourself to death—leaves a huge wake of sadness and destruction.

I see it every day when I am with my friend and his family. They are in so much pain, trying to make sense of losing their loved one. When we are in our addiction or in extreme mental anguish, we think this is the only way out, the only way to experience relief. This is not true: there is help and a solution.

Through the years of my sobriety I have seen good, bad, and tragedy in the lives of others. I often ask *why?* Why do we have to suffer? I do not know the answer, and it is not my responsibility to know.

It is my responsibility to live my life each day being grateful and open to life. To reach out to others I meet and ask, *How are you?*—and truly mean it. I know when I go through the day angry, full of anxiety or just feeling *poor me,* I cannot help anyone. I miss the signals that I need and want to hear to live a full and happy life that serves others.

These days we can be anyone we want to be on social media. People talk less face-to-face. We view our "friends" lives on social media and think we really know how they are feeling.

We take the time to get to know people online to date them, only to find out they are not who they portray themselves to be. Or they disappear after days, weeks or months of correspondence. What are we missing when we spend all this time behind a screen?

Offer a smile, a hello, buy someone a cup of coffee. You never know what kind of impact such a simple act can have on another. When you see someone struggling, help them if you can. If not, call the authorities. We all need to remain safe, but there is always a way to help.

Life is short and precious. Make each day count. I find the best way to make my day complete is to know I'm spreading love and happiness everywhere I go, even to those who do not deserve it. That is the toughest thing to do. But living life this way, you grow.

As Mother Teresa said, "Spread love everywhere you go. Let no one ever come to you without leaving happier."

What I have gone through in my life has taught me many things, most importantly how to live with balance in my life. To live a peaceful life, to love and to be open to love, to be free of self-doubt, and to perform meaningful work. I lived my life thinking that being strong was to never feel pain. Today I know the strongest people feel pain, go through it, and accept it.

I know that those of us who want to change their life can. I am an example of that will. My dream is to live the rest of my days helping those in need. I want others to truly feel alive in their life. This life is all we have; we have one time around. I want to make every second my best.

You can do anything you set your mind to.
BENJAMIN FRANKLIN

ABC PRINCIPLES
TO LIVE A HAPPY LIFE

A — ABSTINENCE FROM ALCOHOL AND DRUGS. When I first quit drinking I felt my life was over. As I thought about my drinking habits during my life, I could not remember the last time I had fun drinking. That realization made it much easier to stay abstinent. I sleep better, I lost weight, and I am not creating pain in the lives of those I love.

B — BELIEVE IN YOURSELF. You can have a life filled with love and happiness. I could not have designed the life I have today because I would not have aimed high enough. Believe in your dreams and work hard to make them happen.

C — COMMUNITY. Human beings need social interaction. Social connection improves physical health and psychological well-being, and also leads to a fifty-percent increased chance of longevity. Find hobbies, meet ups, church, meetings, and volunteer. This made a huge difference in my life. I found activities that I truly love and my life became an adventure.

D – DON'T RUN. Face the problem, the person, or the feeling. Nothing goes away until we face it and deal with it. This can be frightening, but once we resolve the situation, we feel good, which leads to a boost in our self-esteem.

E – EXPERIMENT. Try different things in life. I found true happiness when I tried different jobs, hobbies and food. I was such a creature of habit. When I experimented with different things and had no expectations, it was pure bliss and my confidence grew.

F – FORGIVENESS. This is a difficult one for many. I had to forgive and take one-hundred-percent responsibility for my part in every aspect of my life. I forgive, because I was forgiven by those I hurt the most.

G – GRATITUDE. My favorite. There is always something to be grateful for in our lives. When I am facing deep pain, I look for gratitude. Even where there is the loss of a loved one, I cherish the memories and believe they are at peace. When a relationship ends, I think of the good times and walk away with more knowledge and love in my soul. At the end of a career, I take all I have learned and focus that energy on what I want to do now that I am free. It is all about perception: we can dwell on the bad things or say, "Okay, what is next for me?"

H – HAPPINESS. We all say, "I want to be happy." I had to find what truly made me happy. Deep inside, what is it that makes you happy? Look beyond the material possessions. These are nice to have, but if you are not truly happy inside, they will not mean much to you for long.

True happiness to me is living my purpose and have meaning in my life.

I — **INSPIRATION.** Live life being inspired; that is the key to living with love and vitality. Do what inspires you and be an inspiration in someone else's life. Be ambitious. Aim high and show others they can reach their goals too.

J — **JUST KEEP MOVING FORWARD.** We know what is behind us. We have today to be the best we can be. If we make today a good day, tomorrow has a good chance of being a good day too. Stay in the middle.

K — **KINDNESS.** Spread love and kindness. This is so simple. Kindness can heal wounds faster than anything else I have witnessed. It takes practice to lead your life in a kind manner but it can be done. Express your anger with conversation not conflict. Kindness can change the world.

L — **LIVE, LOVE AND LAUGH.** Live your life free from addiction, guilt and shame. Love yourself and love others. Laugh. I love to laugh, especially at myself. Laughter has healing benefits, increases resilience and reduces stress. Share love and laughter; we all need to feel love!

M — **MEDITATION.** I had such a hard time trying to quiet my mind. Eventually, I could rest and feel the moment, the peace and serenity. I use meditation to focus on what I need to improve in my life or to just listen to the silence. Answers usually come when we are in a relaxed state.

N — **NATURE.** Step out into nature as often as possible. There is evidence that contact with nature has significant positive impact on mental health. Even looking out a window or glancing at photos of nature helps boost your mood. I do not go a day without being in nature.

I become creative in nature and find solutions to my problems on a trail or at the beach. Get out there!

O – **OPEN TO LIFE.** Be open to life and all life offers. Pain has taught us to close ourselves off. When we close ourselves off, we miss out on the good things in life. Go through life with open hands. Give love and be open to receive love.

P – **PERSEVERANCE.** As Winston Churchill said, "If you are going through hell, keep going." To reach your dreams or get through a rough time you must persevere. Never settle. You are worth it and you can achieve your dreams. Keep moving forward.

Q – **QUESTION YOUR INTENTIONS.** When making decisions, I question my motives and actions. Why do I want this and what direction should I take to reach my goals? Questioning my motives clears the path for me. Good questions to ask are: Why do I want this? Am I being honest? Is this good for me?

R – **RELATIONSHIPS.** True happiness and fulfillment comes from within. When we are healthy we attract healthy relationships. Be happy alone so when you find a special person you can both give and receive love. Attract healthy relationships by being healthy. We all have unhealthy relationships that we must keep, maybe an ex or a close relative. Know your limits and set boundaries. Never allow them to pull you back into the madness. Walk away with a smile.

S – **SPIRITUALITY.** I have a strong faith and from that faith my life is filled with peace, love and hope. When I behave in ways that are spiritual, my life is much easier. To me spirituality is being loving and kind to others.

T – **TRUST.** Be trustworthy, have integrity, and be consistent. People can trust me today. This is a gift and I treasure it. I trust others, and if they let me down I learn quickly that this is a person I do not want in my life. There are many good people to let in your life. Do not make excuses for those who break your trust.

U — UNDERSTAND. Learn to listen to understand another person. Do not respond to what they are saying, understand them first. You become more caring and humble. Focusing on understanding has helped me become a better listener.

V — VICTORY. Live your life victorious; you are not a victim. We have a choice to say, "I will no longer be a victim." Do not let something that happened to you in your past continue to dictate your life. Be free and be happy. You are a good person: believe that with all your heart.

W —WONDER. Live your life in constant wonder about what the world offers. We live in a gigantic and gorgeous world. Do not let it pass you by without enjoying every second.

X — XOXO. Kisses and hugs to yourself and those you love. Hugs and kisses boosts your immune system, too. Kisses stimulate the brain to release dopamine, the pleasure hormone. Try it!

Y — YOUNG AT HEART. Have a youthful outlook on life. We are never too old to follow our dreams. Regret is painful. Stay young, fun and adventurous. This is your life—live it with passion.

Z — ZERO TOLERANCE. No time for self-doubt, fear, or unhappiness. Change the conversation in your head. Tell yourself, "I am worth it, I am successful and I am happy!" Focus on the good in life. Whatever you focus on, you attract.

ABOUT THE AUTHOR

Karen Alexander is an author, personal coach, speaker and wellness-travel enthusiast. Born and raised in the Bay Area she raised two beautiful sons, owned and operated a successful business for over thirty-two years, and has helped many create a life of their design.

Karen experienced pain and struggles throughout her lifetime, but has turned her adversities into a life filled with happiness, love and passion. Her mission in life is to help others overcome their struggles so they, too, can live a life of their dreams.

www.ingramcontent.com/pod-product-compliance
Lightning Source LLC
Chambersburg PA
CBHW031536040426
42445CB00010B/561